INTERPRETATIONS OF THE TWO GERMANIES
SECOND EDITION

Studies in European History

General Editor: Richard Overy
Editorial Consultants: John Breuilly
Roy Porter

Interpretations of the Two Germanies

Second Edition

Mary Fulbrook

First published in Great Britain 2000 by
MACMILLAN PRESS LTD
Houndmills, Basingstoke, Hampshire RG21 6XS and London
Companies and representatives throughout the world

A catalogue record for this book is available from the British Library.

ISBN 0–333–66579–1 paperback

First published in the United States of America 2000 by
ST. MARTIN'S PRESS, INC.,
Scholarly and Reference Division,
175 Fifth Avenue, New York, N.Y. 10010

ISBN 0–312–23190–3 (paper)

Library of Congress Cataloging-in-Publication Data
Fulbrook, Mary, 1951–
Interpretations of the two Germanies, 1945–1990 / Mary Fulbrook.–2nd ed.
p. cm.—(Studies in European history)
Includes bibliographical references and index.
ISBN 0–312–23190–3
1. Germany (West)—Politics and government. 2. Germany (East)—Politics and
government. 3. Germany—History—Unification, 1990. 4. Political culture–
Germany. 5. Germany—Economic policyó1945—1990. I. Title. II. Studies in
European history (New York, N.Y.)
DD258.7.F86 2000
943.0876d c21   99–089381

This book is printed on paper suitable for recycling and made from fully managed and
sustained forest sources.

10   9   8   7   6   5   4   3   2   1
09 08 07 06 05 04 03 02 01 00

Printed in Malaysia

Contents

1 Introduction

For most of the late twentieth century the Nazi past tended to overshadow perceptions of Germany and the Germans. But now, with the onset of the twenty-first century, even the two successor states – the Federal Republic of Germany and the German Democratic Republic – are beginning to appear more strange, more distant, curious products of and prime exhibits in a Cold War world which dramatically disappeared with the collapse of communism in 1989–90. The increased historical distance has certainly served to enhance access to the sources of the now defunct state, the GDR; it has not necessarily made for greater consensus on interpretations.

The two Germanies, which coexisted in uneasy opposition and mutual competition for forty years after the defeat of Hitler's Third Reich, represented a remarkable historical experiment. A most unlikely scenario developed in the latter half of the twentieth century: the rump of defeated Nazi Germany was being transformed into two very different entities, capitalist-democratic on the one side and communist on the other. Each appeared, in terms of political stability and economic performance, to be a model example of its type. Moreover the division of Germany (and of Europe and the superpower blocs) seemed an increasingly unquestionable, indeed permanent, feature of the geopolitical landscape. By the late 1980s it was generally recognised that only lip-service need be paid by West Germans to their constitution's preamble committing them to reunification. But then, with the collapse of Soviet bloc communism, the East German revolution of 1989 inaugurated the end of division and the hurtling towards the uneasy unification, on 3 October 1990, of two Germanies that had by now become very different sorts of sociopolitical entity. With unification a new experiment was embarked upon: that of combining a former communist state with a capitalist democracy, in the context of a radically changed post-Cold War Europe.

This double history poses several sets of substantive explanatory problems. The division of Germany, the character of each state, the reasons for the success of West German democracy (particularly in view of the disastrous demise of its Weimar precursor) and the eventual failure of the communist project in the East have all been the focus of heated controversy.

The Federal Republic of Germany and the German Democratic Republic were founded as conscious attempts to develop new forms of state and society, radically breaking with the Nazi past, and based on explicit political ideologies and theories of society. They were in effect tests in reality of opposing theories of how to create a 'good' society. The Federal Republic sought to institutionalise a parliamentary democracy on Anglo-American principles, combined with pre-Nazi German democratic traditions. The GDR, by contrast, was premised on and legitimated by the would-be 'scientific' theories of society embodied in Marxism–Leninism – as currently interpreted by those communists in power.

This historical experiment – this test of social and political theories in reality – was in no sense 'value neutral'. The two Germanies were created by the superpowers as antagonistic, opposing entities: they represented the front line of the Cold War, and the hostile armies of East and West faced each other across the Iron Curtain which ran down the inner frontier of this divided nation.

The two Germanies bristled not only with armaments but also with wholly opposing world views: they painted each other in black and white terms, as friend and foe, as all Good or all Evil; attempts to develop a more differentiated or sympathetic picture of the other camp might be denigrated as a form of fifth columnism. Even the most sober, seemingly objective comparison of the two systems would inevitably raise problems of evaluation in the light of moral–political criteria. For example the formal political democracy and civil liberties of the Federal Republic could easily be favourably contrasted with the obvious political repression of the GDR; but apologists for the latter could point to the real restrictions on freedom for those unable to afford the 'freedom of choice' supposedly offered in the West, while emphasising the egalitarian socioeconomic goals of the East. Inherent in the latter view would be a very different conception of historical dynamics and political priorities than in the pro-Western view.

The very concepts used in political debate were also, of course, those of academic discourse. Words such as 'socialism' and 'communism' are common currency in the cut-and-thrust of contemporary politics – and are not always used with the precision of meaning necessary for scholarly debate. The collapse of neo-Stalinist communist regimes in Eastern Europe in 1989 was often seized upon by Western right-wingers as an opportunity to proclaim the 'triumph of capitalism' or the 'death of socialism', without any attempt to differentiate between democratic socialist ideals on the one hand and perversions of a Marxist–Leninist dictatorship on the other. Indeed the occasion was specifically used for politically inspired analytical confusion – not only among politicians but also within the academic communities.

Although of course constraints and influences on scholarship were very different in East and West during the period of division, inevitably the political animosities of the Cold War period rubbed off on scholarly analyses, and this not only for those Germans most directly affected by division. Much Anglo-American writing on the two Germanies was also, to a greater or lesser degree, affected by one form or another of political bias. And given the backdrop of Auschwitz, debates about the nature of the present were also in many ways political and moral debates about degrees of responsibility for and the extent of 'overcoming' a uniquely reprehensible past.

Although the quantity of factual information available has grown exponentially and the political parameters have changed dramatically, old animosities continue in new forms. Is it possible to interpret the character of the GDR in ways which can be recognised by those who lived through it, or must the interpretations of *Besser-Wessis* (know-it-all Westerners) be accepted? Is the 'Ostalgia' of many East Germans more a reflection of the miseries of what is often experienced as a colonial status in the present than an adequate account of a now idealised past? There is as yet no consensus on interpretations of recent German history.

* * *

This book focuses on interpretations of a few thematic areas of interest. First, we must look at the general types of interpretive framework which have been advanced.

There have been major changes in the parameters of debate since unification. Not only has the collapse of the GDR and the opening of the East German archives led to the unprecedented and immediate availability of vast quantities of previously inaccessible material; the collapse of a state and its incorporation by its former Cold War arch enemy has led to a radical change in interpretative perspectives.

In the years before the fall of the Wall, few Westerners were much interested in the GDR. Since unification there has been an explosion of publications on the GDR. These have been partly driven by the need for information on the part of the politicians, civil servants and members of the business community who rushed in to 'restructure' the newly incorporated provinces of the Federal Republic; partly by the desire to 'know the truth' on the part of those who were, in one way or another, victims of a repressive regime; and partly by a media feeding frenzy, eager for ever new revelations about the compromised past of public figures. Historical research has grown exponentially, with growing numbers of historians scouring the extraordinary richness of the East German archives and reconsidering the intricacies of the workings of a dictatorship at which they could only previously guess. There is as yet no general consensus on interpretations of East German history.

Roughly, one could divide post-unification interpretations into several partially overlapping phases and broad types of analysis. First – particularly in the early 1990s – there was a highly politicised phase characterised by the rapid publication of a great deal of what might be termed 'heroes, victims and villains' literature [see summaries in 1]: eye-witness reports and collections of documents about the 1989 revolution; interviews with and memoirs of both former big-wigs and oppositionalists; sensationalist journalistic 'revelations'; indictments, even by apparently sober academics, of links between state, Stasi and prominent literary figures or supposedly moral institutions such as the Churches [see for example 1, 2, 11, 54, 74, 117, 159, 160, 163]. This wave was then partially subsumed by the publication of supposedly more 'scientific' overviews and analyses, which nevertheless often also had a quite explicit moral and political message and were by no means uncontentious in explanatory framework or implications [for example 16, 17]. Some of these emanated from scholars who had been prevented from full careers by their unwillingness to make all the necessary compromises in the GDR; others came from continuing 'Cold Warriors' in the West [see for two notable examples 140, 162].

There have also been increasing numbers of specialist monographs, with a marked shift in emphasis towards less condemnatory approaches. Many of these contributions will be taken into account in the chapters which follow. Notable too is a move away from a focus on the structures of power and repression towards more all-encompassing approaches, including an emphasis on social and cultural history. The Zentrum für Zeithistorische Forschung in Potsdam played a major role in stimulating much of this research, and providing for fruitful interaction between Western and Eastern scholars [see for some examples 8, 9, 18, 84, 94, 95, 107, 108].

Once the early excitement over the wave of archival revelations had somewhat subsided, some historians have began to call for an escape from the 'fetishism of the documents' (or the rush for the archives, in the assumption that all the inner secrets will thus be revealed) and to adopt a more thoughtful approach to analysis of the GDR. A few have even attempted to reconsider the writings of GDR historians in less condemnatory tones, although on the whole Marxist–Leninist versions of history have been condemned to the historical dustbin along with the state in which they constituted the 'legitimatory discourse' [see for some examples in a rapidly growing field, 46, 85, 158]. Even the German parliament made an extensive attempt, through its commission of inquiry (*Enquetekommission*), to 'come to terms' with the history of the GDR in a series of hearings with specialists [40]. This prompted a parallel set of 'alternative' interpretations on the part of the communist successor party, the PDS [see for example the first volume, 100]. The field remains a minefield of disagreements and controversies, rooted in part in political differences (which, it should be noted, cross the inner-German divide) and in part in differences of theoretical paradigm and approach.

It cannot be said that this explosion of interest in and re-evaluation of the GDR, and of its erstwhile official interpreters, has been accompanied by anything like a comparable re-examination of West German history (not to mention a re-examination of its pre-1990 analysts, who have by and large remained in positions of academic security). However some more subtle changes have taken place, even in the field of West German history. The collapse of the GDR prompted a renewed interest in the implications of, for example, 'German–German policies' (was 1990 a vindication of Adenauer's 'magnet theory', delayed by *Ostpolitik* – or was it only possible as a result of détente?) The peaceful reunification of Germany removed taboos on previous confessions of belief in the nation and permitted a resurgence in the use of this term [see the somewhat overstated indictment in 13]. There was also a more positive interpretation of the achievements of the West German constitution in founding a stable and secure democracy [in English, see for example the essay by Kocka in 60]. At the same time attempts began to be made to explore the possibility of developing a single narrative of the 'double history of Germany', integrating the East German past into the history of the Federal Republic, from the vantage point of a unified state [8]. The implicit 'end of history' appeared now to have moved from 1945 to 1990, finally prompting even cautious historians to look across the watershed of 1945 and creep through the occupation period into the 1950s, leading to some highly interesting reinterpretations of this formative period of postwar Germany. Thus if not quite on the cataclysmic scale of re-evaluations of the GDR, pre-1990s West Germany was also the focus of some detailed historical re-evaluation.

Marxist approaches have clearly fallen out of fashion since the collapse of communism, and right-wing interpretations are enjoying a new popularity. Many current academic debates, however, have longer roots (particularly when referring to Western interpretations) and not all pre-1989 discussions have become irrelevant. Let us look, very briefly, at what was on offer in the way of interpretations prior to 1989. The Iron Curtain on the ground was reflected, unsurprisingly, by dramatic differences in the character of scholarly interpretations.

Analyses of GDR history and society written by East Germans prior to 1989 may be divided into several groups. First, there were the official published histories, specifically intended as forms of legitimation of the rule of the SED [in English, see for example 76]. As the SED's self-understanding changed, so too did the emphases in official histories. East German official analyses of West Germany tended to be simple denunciations of capitalist imperialism, intended to foster the 'friend/foe' mentality of the Cold War. Given their political intent, such 'histories' must be read essentially as ideological documents. This is less true of the second category: the often unpublished analyses carried out by both academic historians and sociologists in various research institutes (such as the Institut für Meinungsforschung, or the Zentralinstitut für Jugendforschung), and also the surveys of public opinion, social problems and so on carried out by organisations such as the FDGB (The League of Free German Trade Unions), the FDJ (Free German Youth), the DFD (The Democratic Women's League) and, not least, the Stasi (The State Security Service). Although all such analyses have to be read with appropriate caution, it should be borne in mind that such unpublished analyses were driven by a vital political interest in identifying real problems with a degree of accuracy in the interests of effective policy making and political control. A third category is that of dissident analyses. As the writings of dissidents such as Rudolf Bahro, Robert Havemann, Rolf Henrich and Franz Loeser reveal, there was potential for much broader public debate on the nature of the GDR. Imaginative literature was also often a form of social commentary in the GDR.

Given the historical fate of the GDR and the victory of Western theoretical approaches in the world of academia, virtually all such analyses are now generally treated as primary sources rather than as academically significant approaches in their own right. While many ex-GDR authors would readily concede that they had to make concessions to political pressures and constraints, there is nevertheless for many former established GDR scholars a degree of difficulty in declaring one's previous life's work to have been essentially worthless, and often also having to take early retirement or unemployment. At the same time there has been considerable resentment among those who refused to conform sufficiently to make any career within the GDR, and now feel doubly excluded from the new, Western-dominated landscape of East German academia. These kinds of resentments certainly play a role in continuing differences of interpretation of the GDR, as well as bitter controversies about who should have an institutional and professional basis for writing GDR history [see particularly 47].

7

Western analyses (both West German and Anglo-American) of the two Germanies were, and continue to be, characterised by a far greater diversity of approach, given the freer conditions of debate and publication. Nevertheless it is remarkable how even in the pre-1990 West the broad development of approaches correlated not only with changes in the two entities under study, but also with changes in the political climate of study. In the 1950s, for example, the GDR was a visibly repressive regime, encapsulated in the then widely accepted concept of 'totalitarianism' – which also served very neatly to establish the similarity of dictatorships of left and right, communism and Nazism, and to establish the 'democratic' credentials of post-Nazi West Germany. Both the changing nature of the GDR in the 1960s and a more pluralistic political climate in the West contributed to the diversification of approaches among Western analysts in the 1960s. The emphasis on the supposed powers of science and technology in both Western and communist states gave rise to a new focus on 'modernisation' and debates about the possible convergence of 'industrial societies', the level of economic development being seen as a more important determining factor than differences in political ideology. The age of technocrats and 'new' middle classes seemed to be dawning in both East and West. While theories of totalitarianism for a time fell out of fashion, they were not replaced by a single, universally accepted alternative. Western approaches to the GDR in the 1970s and 1980s were on the whole far less politicised and condemnatory in tone, echoing the changed political climate of the post-*Ostpolitik* era of détente. Some Western scholars after 1990 have castigated this more open-minded approach as a woolly liberalism serving to sustain an illegitimate dictatorship [72].

As far as Western analyses of West Germany were concerned, views diverged to a considerable degree. Given Germany's turbulent political past, a lot of research was devoted to analysing the functioning of West Germany's political institutions, the evolution of the party system and aspects of political culture [33, 34, 48, 101, 182]. West Germans were probably subjected to more public opinion surveys than any other population in the world [134, 147]. Early fears began to give way to the more admiring attempts of certain political scientists to unlock the secrets of what was increasingly perceived as a 'model state' [151]. The apparently highly successful record of West German industrial relations and economic policy management came under increasing scrutiny, as did West German federalism, relations with the European Community and international relations [see for a range of analyses and summaries 171, 172, 173].

At the same time, from the late 1960s a variety of neo-Marxist critiques of the supposedly 'neofascist' form of 'late capitalism' proliferated. Although a minority tried to put theory into 'praxis' and turned to violence, most restricted themselves to more arcane, intellectual critiques of the perceived shortcomings of West German bourgeois democracy. Furthermore most Western radicals did not consider the repressive regime in East Germany as in any way representing a model of truly humanist democratic socialism. Although neo-Marxist approaches were very much less fashionable by the 1980s, their unexamined heritage – in terms of, for example, looking behind formal political structures to examine the real distribution of power and the role of important economic interest groups in processes of policy formation – should not be underestimated. And on the right, Cold War approaches smacking more of the flavour of the 1950s than of the period of superpower détente were still appearing at the end of the 1980s [7]. Between these extremes there were continuing academic debates on a range both of specific issues and of more general approaches. And public debate over – indeed almost obsession with – the nature of West German national identity and political culture was accompanied by a continuing trickle of journalistic accounts of the 'other Germany', about which many West Germans knew comparatively little (and had even less interest in). In general one might want to summarise approaches to the two Germanies by Western scholars in terms of a plurality of theoretical approaches and lively (sometimes vitriolic) debates on particular issues.

Most analyses of recent German history are, almost inevitably, heavily laden with a penumbra of political associations and implications. On the other hand it must be emphasised that historical analysis is not simply political assertion: for all the arguments of the more relativist postmodernists (which there is not the space to explore here!) there are standards of empirical evidence against which claims and assertions may be tested. Different questions and different concepts will of course lead to the gathering and categorisation of different kinds of data; and all the evidence required for a definitive answer to any particular question may not, for one reason or another, necessarily be available. But in the chapters that follow we must consider, in respect of each area of controversy, where the balance of available evidence should lead us by way of any more general, empirically grounded conclusion.

2 Historical Development

Periodisation is a convenient framework for the retrospective imposition of intellectual order on the flow of events and trends. A narrative structure with distinct acts and scenes is imposed on the richness and diversity of historical material available to the historian. Sometimes turning points are obvious: there are key dates which stand out as denoting major turning points, beginnings or ends. But historians are often concerned with identifying and explaining longer trends of continuity or more gradual processes of change. Historians working in different theoretical traditions will tend to impose rather different categories on whatever they select and define as discrete historical periods. And it is often only with the benefit of hindsight that certain developments or events stand out as important.

Periodisation is, however, not just an idle game, an essentially arbitrary imposition by historians imagining and reconstructing a past they cannot know in its entirety. It makes a difference to or is intrinsically embedded in the kind of overall interpretation that is being presented. For example books such as Mitter and Wolle's *Untergang auf Raten* [140] (roughly, 'Decline and Fall in Stages') imply that the GDR was essentially 'doomed from the start'; the end was prefigured already in 1953. Others would, however, represent GDR history in terms of a '*rise* and fall', with a possible 'golden age' in the 1960s and/or 1970s [59, 94]. This periodisation would then imply quite different questions about 'what went wrong' and what might have been done to prevent eventual collapse: the focus would not be, as in Mitter and Wolle's account, on a constant state of 'latent civil war', but rather on initial stabilisation and then on later destabilisation, analysing the specific combinations of factors in the 1970s and 1980s that led into 1989.

11

There are thus important questions relating not purely to periodisation but also, vitally, to the characterisation and explanation of the histories of each of the two states.

The succession of governments and political leaders forms a very standard, traditional means of periodisation; implicit in this approach is the notion that the personality of the leader and/or the political complexion of the government is the most important factor. Thus pre-1990 West German history would be divided according to individual chancellorships or the general complexion of the government (the conservative-dominated phase of 1949–66, the 'Grand Coalition' of 1966–69, the social-liberal coalition of 1969–82, then back to conservative-liberal government). Similarly a straight political history approach would subdivide the GDR into three periods: that of Walter Ulbricht's leadership from 1949 to 1971; the Honecker era, from his accession to power in 1971 until the revolution of 1989; and the period of collapse of communist rule, transition to democratic government and ultimately unification with the West in 1989–90.

However quite different criteria might be applied by historians with another angle of interest. Marxist historians in the GDR on the whole considered that the dates of political leaders were less important than what they wanted to designate as specific phases of societal development. The official illustrated history of the GDR published in 1985, for example, distinguishes the following periods: antifascist democratic transformation, 1945–49; building the foundations of socialism, 1949–61; on the way to a 'developed socialist society', 1961–70; and the further formation of the developed socialist society, 1971–84. Other GDR histories subdivided GDR history in relation to major party conferences. Periodisation could be altered according to changing political priorities [see also 187].

Social, cultural and economic historians would, however, see other periodisations as important for their purposes. There has, for example, for some time been a debate about the putative rule of the Third Reich in the 'modernisation' of German society; but some historians have emphasised continuities in the West German economy and society until the 1960s, which many perceive as a crucial decade of social and cultural change (whatever the importance of earlier changes in the political context). These discussions have by no means been resolved.

12

There are also questions concerning the extent to which there are interconnections, parallels and asymmetries in the two histories taken together. Since 1990 more strenuous efforts have been made by German historians to write recent German history as one narrative rather than ignoring – as many pre-unification histories tended to do – almost entirely the history of the 'wrong side of the Wall' [see for example the introduction to 8]. Clearly one can explore each of these questions in its own right: the impact of West German *Ostpolitik* on the GDR; the ways in which both German governments responded to and dealt with common trends and challenges in a changing international political, economic and cultural system; differences relating to their respective Cold War contexts, or particular events which impacted primarily on one side or the other – all these are legitimate questions under the general heading of periodisation.

Bearing these qualifications in mind, for the moment a rough, six-phase periodisation may be a convenient framework for introducing specific historical debates and broader interpretations of patterns of development.

(i) Occupation and Division, 1945–49

The Allies had no clear idea during and immediately after the war concerning what should be done with defeated Germany. Although quite radical plans for its dismemberment and reconstitution as a number of smaller states had been mooted during the war, such a scheme had never actually been approved. The eventual division of Germany four years later was an *ad hoc*, unintended result of the emerging Cold War between the superpowers, rather than the outcome of conscious Allied policies for Germany. Even after the formal foundation of two German states in 1949, the question of whether the unity of Germany in some form might yet be salvaged remained open, certainly until Stalin's initiative in 1952, and in some senses (including the normal commitment to reunification in West Germany's 'provisional' constitution) for a considerable while thereafter. [For interesting discussion of a wide range of issues and good selections of documents in German, see 103 and 177.]

13

On the part of the Americans and British there was a dramatic transformation in policy orientation, from an early, rather draconian and punitive approach to an emphasis on rebuilding at least the areas of Germany under their control. By the spring of 1946 it had become clear to both powers that Germany – and particularly the German economy – must be rebuilt rather than ravaged. Britain was barely able to feed her own population, let alone sustain her former enemies, the Germans; and in the USA the perceived dangers of communism were beginning to outweigh the desire to punish former Nazis. So there was a major turnaround in policy, symbolised eventually by the input of Marshall Aid and the defence and support of the Western zones in Germany. West Germany became an ally in the fight to defend 'freedom and democracy' against the evils of 'totalitarian' communism. This was particularly so when, after the Western currency reform on 20 June 1948, the Soviets sought to cut off West Berlin from all road, rail and water links with the West. During the 'Berlin blockade', which lasted from 24 June 1948 to 12 May 1949, the Western allies flew in planeload after planeload of supplies, and in the process transformed West Berlin from a symbol of Nazism and militarism into the last outpost of Western democracy. Meanwhile the desire of the French to strip their zone and seek maximum reparations was finally brought into line with American and British policies, with the French entering into a 'trizonia' in April 1949, only shortly before the creation of the Federal Republic out of the three Western zones.

No doubt Stalin would in principle have preferred the whole of Germany to be under communist control. But the drastic dismantling of East German industry and the shipping back to the Soviet Union of reparations in kind in the early postwar period suggested that, at least initially, Stalin was keeping his options open and taking what he could while the going was good. Nevertheless the Russians also sought from the outset to transform their zone of occupation into something more akin to the Soviet mould [on the twists and turns of the Soviet occupation on the ground, see particularly 142]. Politically, communists were immediately installed into key positions [still relevant is 121]. There was an early and dramatic socioeconomic revolution: in the land reform of September 1945 estates of over 100 hectares and those allegedly belonging to former Nazis were confiscated and

14

redistributed, while in 1946 nationalisation measures were applied to industry and finance. Further measures over the next two years culminated in very close communist control over most areas of life and political activity by the summer of 1948, when the overt Stalinisation of East German politics was effected (see further below).

Although historians are still divided over the question of whether American perceptions of the Soviet threat were realistic or exaggerated, analysis of the actual steps through which the division of Germany proceeded reveals that the Western powers repeatedly took initiatives to which Soviet measures came largely in response. Moreover division came about largely out of the power-political and economic considerations of the victorious Allies, and under conditions which might have been thought less than propitious for conducting historical experiments. This must be borne in mind when we consider the actual results of the 'experiment'. It is also important to remember the role of the Germans themselves in division: for one thing, in cooperating with the respective Allies and acquiescing in the processes leading to division; and for another – not least in importance – through having first unleashed the war which had brought about total defeat and a determination on the part of the Allies to ensure that Germany could never again pose such a danger.

Politically coloured arguments have also focused on broader interpretations of the effects of Allied policies, particularly in the Western zones. Was 1945 really the 'zero hour' which many West Germans liked later to proclaim; was there really a fresh start? Analysis suggests a high degree of continuity as far as both personnel and economic structures were concerned in West Germany, although of course the political framework was radically changed. This relates to the issue of 'missed opportunities': would alternative policies really have been feasible?

Some historians have pointed rather disapproving fingers at the American and British proclivity for disbanding indigenous antifascist groups ('antifas'); for hindering the development of trade union and social democratic organisations while aiding those of employers and right-wingers; for blocking socialisation measures supported by some German regional governments; for turning de-Nazification into a tangle of bureaucratic procedures, encouraging a degree of aggrieved self-justification and white-washing rather than any real confrontation with the past, and allowing the 'big fish' to escape while only the 'small fry' were netted; and for failing to effect land reform, or radical reform of the education system. Others have suggested that the Western Allies did a good job in difficult conditions. On this view, there was only minority support for antifascist groups; there would have been little benefit to be gained from nationalising a ruined economy; failing to support employers and technical experts would have only prolonged the chaotic conditions which would have allowed communism to spread; and unwillingness to forgive former Nazis and accept them back into society would have provided a breeding ground for discontent from the right. In support of this view – and whatever the moral rectitude of the former view – an appeal might be made to the very different conditions obtaining after German defeat in the First World War – with all the serious consequences which followed.

As far as the Soviet zone is concerned, there are comparable debates. Many important areas remain the subject of contention, particularly in connection with the imposition of hard-line communism. Why, for example, did the SPD finally accede to a forced merger with the KPD to form the SED (Socialist Unity Party) in April 1946? Could more effective opposition have been put up in any way to increased communist control of other political and social organisations, or to the effective Stalinisation of the SED itself (as a 'party of a new type') in 1948? How did local populations actually experience and respond to the dramatic changes affecting their lives, and seek strategies to adapt and survive under new conditions? The opening up of the archives has led to a wealth of new knowledge on such questions.

What is clear is that by the time of the formal foundation of the two republics in 1949, despite very clear differences between the zones, the future was by no means preordained. Few could have predicted at this time that division would last so long, or produce two such different states and societies.

There was, it is true, something of an economic upturn on the West German side; but opinion polls reveal that a high proportion of West Germans were still antidemocratic in political orientation, and prone to grumble about the miseries of everyday life and the unfairness of de-Nazification procedures. On the Soviet side, only a minority of the population were committed communists: most were hoping that the present arrangements would prove to be transitory, and in the meantime tried to make the best of things – or left for the West. Moreover with the changed boundaries of postwar Germany literally millions of people were on the move – whether expelled from former eastern homelands, trekking westwards or seeking as displaced persons to return home and try to rebuild broken lives. Others were simply trying to shape some sort of existence, to survive among the ruins and rubble, and were more concerned about the return of their own loved ones than the political future of Germany.

(ii) Crystallisation, 1949–61

Many Germans in the early postwar period hoped for a new beginning in German politics: they harboured visions of a 'Third Way', a form of democratic socialism that would lie between the devil of Stalinist communism and the deep blue sea of conservative capitalism. On some views, crucial opportunities were missed and the future of Germany might have been cast very differently. Although related to the issue of whether Germany would be divided or united – many adherents of third way views hoped for a united, neutral, non-militarised Germany – this question is also distinct. Even given that there were to be two Germanies, neither might have turned out quite the way it did. At the beginning of the 1950s the respective successes of Konrad Adenauer in the West and Walter Ulbricht in the East could not have been predicted with any certainty. Both had to deal, in different ways, with a range of challenges to their regimes.

The controversial role of Konrad Adenauer – who in 1949 was only narrowly elected chancellor, by one vote, of a coalition government – was highly important in determining the course of subsequent West German history [for a variety of interpretations see 5, 7, 145, 154, 164]. A conservative Rhineland Catholic, he was prepared to jettison the (predominantly Protestant) East Germans to their fate under Soviet domination in favour of speedy integration into Western economic, political and military alliances. Adenauer's orientations corresponded very closely with those of the Western allies, particularly the USA, as for example in their unwillingness to treat seriously Stalin's note of March 1952

17

proposing an apparently genuinely intended scheme for reunification [177]. America's main political consideration – the 'containment' of communism – went along with economic considerations, in particular the expansion of markets in Europe. This too in numerous ways aided Adenauer's position. The rapid economic growth or 'economic miracle' of the 1950s (based not only on Marshall Aid) played a major role in anchoring public support for the new democratic regime in the western part of divided, defeated Germany and in the growth of popular support for the CDU/CSU. Nevertheless Adenauer's chancellorship was not without its problems. His resignation finally came in 1963, under rather a cloud, in the wake of the 'Spiegel affair' of autumn 1962. There was also criticism of Adenauer's willingness to incorporate former Nazis into the new, bourgeois, materialist and self-satisfied Federal Republic while suppressing initiatives for radical reform and real breaks with a compromised past [see for example 54, 61, 79]. And Adenauer's autocratic style of government gave rise to a new political concept, 'chancellor democracy'.

In the GDR, Ulbricht faced serious challenges, both to his own leadership and to the rule of the party. Ironically he was narrowly saved from machinations in Moscow to remove him from power, following Stalin's death in the spring of 1953, by the uprising of 17 June 1953 [for a variety of interpretations of the uprising see 6, 43, 73, 114]. This in the event provided him with the opportunity to build on an earlier purge of party membership and to effect the exclusion of many former social democrats from the ranks of the SED. In 1956 and again in 1958 Ulbricht successfully dealt with factionalism in the higher ranks of the SED, such that by the end of the 1950s he was in command of a well-disciplined party. Moreover the institutions of the state were increasingly brought under party control, as with the abolition of the *Länder* (provinces with their own regional governments) in 1952 and their replacement by smaller *Bezirke* (districts), and with the abolition in 1958 of the upper house of parliament, which had nominally represented the regions. Ministries too were adapted to ensure effective communist control of all areas of policy. Nevertheless recent research suggests that the translation of central policies into realities at the grass-roots level was often less than effective, and the leaders of the SED could by no means fully rely on a network of loyal local functionaries [59].

Radical transformation of the East German economy proved less successful. Central planning and a focus on heavy industry were both inefficient and detrimental to consumer interests, while the bouts of collectivisation of agriculture in 1952–53 and 1960 created major dislocations in the food supply and occasioned mass disaffection. Continued haemorrhaging of young, skilled labour as thousands fled to the West in search of better prospects, led to the eventual erection of the Berlin Wall in August 1961.

For all the dramatic differences in substance there are striking formal similarities between the histories of the two German states in the 1950s. On the domestic front, oppositional forces in each Germany were disadvantaged by the roles of the USA and USSR respectively, as well as lacking, for one reason or another, adequate domestic support for their programmes. Neutralist and antimilitarist sentiments in West Germany did not accord well with American plans for NATO, while the SPD's inherited Marxist rhetoric appeared a serious electoral liability – particularly in the face of the actualities of communist rule in the GDR – and was ultimately jettisoned in the Bad Godesberg meeting of 1959. In the East, returning exiles and others of a humanist Marxist persuasion soon found force and repression a rather serious obstacle to their hopes. Explanations of the failures of dissenting forces or proponents of a 'third way' – the desire for a form of democratic socialism, rather than either Stalinist dictatorship or conservative capitalism – on both sides have been various: while some castigate the alleged failure of nerve or strategy, others emphasise overwhelming obstacles; yet others suggest that such visions were unrealistic to start with.

As far as the international situation of the two Germanies was concerned, both superpowers had effectively recognised the stalemate of the *status quo* by the mid 1950s. Both Germanies were accorded full sovereignty in 1955 (with certain residual allied rights) and gained their own armed forces. Both Germanies were incorporated as important partners into wider international networks: the GDR into the Warsaw Pact and Comecon, the Federal Republic into Nato and as a founder member of the European Economic Community (EEC, later EC and eventually EU). Gradually each German state worked its passage from subordinate former enemy to respected ally and partner in its sphere of alliance. But the issue of reunification remained. The Federal Republic was committed by its constitution to work for reunification, and under the so-called Hallstein doctrine refused to recognise the legitimacy of the GDR (or 'the zone') or maintain diplomatic relations with countries, other than the USSR, that did recognise the GDR. The latter, for its part, maintained that it was the West which had taken all the initiative over division and now represented the imperialist aggressor and counterrevolutionary force. [For an interesting analysis of the ways in which their respective domestic political structures affected German–German relations see 131.]

(iii)   The 1960s: Decade of Transition

In many ways the 1960s represent a decade of transition in both Germanies.

In East Germany the building of the Berlin Wall and the ensuing effective 'house arrest' of its entire population paradoxically inaugurated a somewhat easier phase as far as domestic policies were concerned. On the one hand Ulbricht could relax a little with an assured labour supply; on the other, recognising that there was no longer an easy way out, people had to make an effort to come to terms with and make the best of the state of affairs that they had to live with. This change in the GDR's domestic atmosphere corresponded with some important shifts in policy. In the economic sphere, the introduction of the 'New Economic System' partially decentralised the economy and introduced certain incentives, along with a higher degree of responsibility for individuals at intermediate levels. The education system was expanded and a higher value was placed on technical experts, who began to feel they had a stake in what became known, following the seminal works of Ludz, as a 'career-oriented achievement society' [124, 125, 126]. In 1968, a new constitution – introduced with much public fanfare and pretence at popular consultation – recognised the very real changes which had occurred in the GDR, such that it was no longer constitutionally comparable to the Federal Republic. The 'leading role' of the Marxist–Leninist party, the SED, was now officially enshrined, and all formal freedoms were hedged with the precondition that they proceeded from the basis of socialism – as defined by the party. It seems, too, that the organs of state were functioning more smoothly, such that unrest in 1968 was effectively nipped in the bud before it could develop into anything like a popular uprising on the lines of 1953. Ulbricht's role in the 1960s has recently been subjected to revision. His reputation as an old guard neo-Stalinist is being replaced by cautious attempts to cast him in the role of at least a qualified reformer [71, 95]. There was clearly a new flexibility and stabilisation in the GDR of the 1960s. If this shift in interpretation of the later Ulbricht era is generally accepted, then closer attention will need to be paid to the failures of the Honecker leadership to tackle effectively the political and, particularly, the economic problems of the period after *Ostpolitik*, when the GDR enjoyed an accepted role on the international stage. More generally the 'doomed from the start' interpretation would need to be dropped in favour of the 'rise and fall' version of GDR history.

In the Federal Republic, too, but in rather different ways, the 1960s were to be a key decade of transition. The 'economic miracle' or rapid take-off of the early years came to an end in the sense that West Germany's economic performance began to normalise, or fall into line with that of other West European countries. There were even moments of faltering, as in the mini-recession of 1965–66, which brought Ludwig Erhard's government to an end and inaugurated the 'Grand Coalition'.

Politically the decade saw tumultuous changes. The materialism, the apparent desire to build for the future and kick over the traces of the past, was subjected to vehement attack by a new, younger generation who challenged the dubious moral rectitude of many of their parents' generation. '1968' came to stand for a dramatic confrontation with the politics, culture and morality of the older generation [in English, and for an international perspective on 1968, see 51]. By the late 1960s there was a political polarisation of new left against 'bourgeois materialist' right, of young against old.

These changes were confirmed with the first major change of government after twenty years of conservative rule (under only three chancellors) in West Germany. With the coming to power in 1969 of a social democratic–liberal coalition government there was an SPD chancellor for the first time since 1928–30, signalling a new era in West German history. Under Willy Brandt *Ostpolitik* was inaugurated, culminating in the mutual recognition of the two Germanies in 1972.

If one looks at the patterns of social continuity and change a rather different set of double transitions can be seen. The GDR saw a dramatic social revolution in the first two decades of its existence, with major changes in the socioeconomic structure, the dismantling of old bases of privilege and the rapid upward mobility of political conformists from worker and peasant backgrounds. In the subsequent two decades this new pattern began to reproduce itself. In the Federal Republic, by contrast, the continuities across the divide of 1945 only began to face serious challenges in the 1960s, with educational reforms and a changed public climate inaugurating a more open and 'Westernised' society in the 1970s and 1980s.

(iv)   The 'Established Phase', c. 1972–89

It did not seem impossible that with the passage of time the two Germanies would grow so far apart that in future they would seem as foreign to each other as to Austria.

In West Germany, parliamentary government was sufficiently institutionalised and flexible to cope with a range of challenges in the 1970s. There were serious problems connected with organised terrorism, particularly on the part of the Red Army Faction, a tiny band of left-wing terrorists who engaged in arson attacks and the murder of prominent industrialists and politicians. Despite some fears about restrictions on democratic freedom of speech and organisation and the increasing powers of the state, West German democracy survived intact. The growth of citizens' initiative movements during the 1970s and the entry into national politics of a new party, the Greens, even indicated the broadening nature of this democracy. In the economically troubled years following the early 1970s – with oil crises and world recession creating serious difficulties for most European economies, Western as well as Eastern – the economy of the Federal Republic was remarkably resilient. As far as the welfare state, social institutions and industrial relations of West Germany in the 1970s were concerned, again there appeared to be some basis for the claim of *Modell Deutschland* ('model Germany') [see for example 151]. Despite increasing labour relations problems, rising unemployment and budgetary difficulties in the 1980s, the West German 'social market economy' continued to earn the widespread admiration of other West European democracies whose economic performance was less resilient to world recession.

Similarly Honecker's GDR seemed in the 1970s to be a bastion of the Eastern bloc, its economy more successful than the economies of its neighbours, its communist rule less threatened by popular challenges to the regime than were the governments of neighbouring Poland or Czechoslovakia. Honecker's proclaimed 'unity of economic and social policy', his emphasis on consumer satisfaction today rather than utopia tomorrow and his relaxation of restrictions in certain spheres (initially culture, and from the late 1970s religion) also seemed to point the way forward to an at least acceptable form of social compact with the citizens of the GDR. Seen by some as 'Moscow's German ally' [27; see also 28], the GDR was generally regarded as the most stable and productive state in the Eastern bloc. Moreover in the course of improved relations between the two Germanies in the 1980s – culminating in Honecker's visit to West Germany in 1987 – the GDR seemed to be carving out a certain distinctive space for itself in relation both to the USSR and to the West.

But there were also, in both Germanies, critical voices and tendencies towards change. With the 1979 decision to station nuclear missiles on German soil, peace campaigners in East and West became increasingly active; environmentalists raised issues of international pollution to a central agenda; and of course the international context (and particularly the interests and capacities for action of the Soviet Union) were changing too. In West Germany the political system was sufficiently flexible to incorporate voices for change. While the return to conservative government in 1982 was accompanied by a 'turning' (*Wende*) towards the right in the 1980s, there were notable continuities in economic and foreign policy (not least in the person of FDP Foreign Minister Hans Dietrich Genscher). Such flexibility was not, however, a feature of the gerontocratic Honecker government of the 1980s. Increasing economic difficulties combined with growing challenges from a tiny minority of oppositional political activists in a changed international climate rendered SED rule in the 1980s far less stable than it had been in the previous decade. So the 'established phase' was by no means static.

(v)   The Collapse of the GDR, 1989–90

Was the collapse of the GDR the inevitable consequence of internal strains and domestic tensions; or did a *deus ex machina*, the leader of the USSR from 1985, Mikahil Gorbachev, simply pull the rug from under Honecker's feet? The collapse of communist government in the GDR has been interpreted variously as a revolution from below, an implosion from above or a collapse of the system from without. Different factors were clearly important at different times [on the end of the GDR see for example 39, 59, 67, 70, 88, 92, 93, 99, 130, 132, 149, 195].

The accession of Mikhail Gorbachev to power in the Soviet Union had clearly inaugurated a totally new era in communist politics, with the new slogans of 'openness' and 'restructuring' permitting liberalisation processes in a number of Soviet bloc states. In the early summer of 1989 a reforming regime in Hungary began to dismantle the fortified border with Austria, providing a hole in the Iron Curtain through which East Germans could escape. The growing stream of refugees posed a major crisis and embarrassment for the GDR regime, which was preparing to celebrate its fortieth anniversary, underlining the essential bankruptcy of any claim to legitimacy on the part of Honecker's government. Meanwhile domestic forces began to exert pressure from within the GDR on the ageing leadership. While dissidents helped to found the New Forum and other new political pressure groups, and organised mass demonstrations in favour of change, at the same time reformists in the ruling SED itself, who had been frustrated by Honecker's resistance to Gorbachev's ideas, began to consider the possibility of introducing certain reforms from above.

In the event, replacing Honecker by Egon Krenz on 18 October 1989 and announcing a limited series of reforms failed either to stem the flow of refugees or to quell the rising tide of protests on the streets. The final concession – the announcement on 9 November 1989 of unrestricted travel to the West – precipitated a major turning-point. With the breaching of the Berlin Wall the floodgates were opened. In the following weeks and months it became increasingly clear – even to those reformers who had wanted to democratise a still independent, socialist GDR – that once open to the lures and competition of the West the GDR would no longer be viable. With surprising speed the SED renounced its claim to a monopoly on power. Following a short period under the 'round-table' government under the leadership of the moderate communist Hans Modrow, elections were held on 18 March 1990. An alliance of conservative parties (supported by the Western ruling CDU, whose leader, Chancellor Kohl, had come out in support of an economically non-viable proposal for currency union on a one-to-one basis) won the day.

Currency union on 1 July 1990 precipitated the collapse of the East German economy, with snowballing unemployment figures exacerbating the personal strains and uncertainties of East Germans in a world in turmoil [on economic aspects see the wide-ranging account in 39]. After the completion of complex international negotiations in the 'two-plus-four' talks (the two Germanies and the four victorious powers from the Second World War) and ratification by the states involved in the Conference on Security and Co-operation in Europe (CSCE), unification of the two Germanies was formally celebrated at midnight on 2–3 October 1990 [for a chronological account of the diplomacy of unification, narrowly defined, see 178]. The GDR had ceased to exist, becoming absorbed as a series of newly reconstituted *Länder* in an enlarged Federal Republic [for mixed international reactions to these events see 87].

As well as considering the relative importance of different factors – such as domestic dissidence – within these few months, longer-term questions also arise. Would the collapse of the GDR have been averted if Honecker had taken much earlier decisive action – from the late 1970s or early 1980s – with respect to the economy? [Cf. the discussions in 39 and 113.] Would it have happened if Honecker had heeded Gorbachev's advice to inaugurate reforms, or indeed if he had stepped down in favour of a more reformist leader? What might a post-1989 GDR have looked like if West Germany had not remained constitutionally committed to reunification and East Germans had not had automatic right of citizenship in the West? Although these are hypothetical questions, they may help not only to sharpen our awareness of the contingency of historical events but also to clarify whether we think the GDR was intrinsically and inevitably 'doomed to fail', or whether specific factors contributed more than others to its collapse.

(vi)   The End of the Two Germanies? United Germany in the 1990s

It did not take very long to realise that what was effected by the merger in 1990 was less the reunification of two halves torn asunder than the unification of two very different sociopolitical, cultural and economic entities [see for example 135, 149, 133]. It was clear from the outset that matters would be very different for the citizens of the ex-GDR – as indeed they had hoped when democratically expressing their desire for unification with the West. It was less clear, however, that despite retention of the old West German constitution the new Federal Republic would not simply replicate, on a larger scale, the old.

A number of areas have been the focus of attention [see for example 172, 173]: the new international role and responsibilities of the Federal Republic, thrown into sharp relief at a very early date by the Gulf War of 1991; the changed parameters of European integration, and Germany's economic and political interests in relation to a broadening or deepening of the European Union; the apparent resurgence of waves of right-wing extremism and xenophobia [cf. 120]; the persistence of divisions between and mutual stereotyping of *Ossis* and *Wessis*; and continued debates about 'mastering the past', which were given a new twist by debates on overcoming the 'second German dictatorship'. In a radically altered European context, opening out to a dramatically transformed Eastern Europe and with deepening integration in the West (the Maastricht Treaty of 1992, the Schengen Agreement on borders of 1995, the introduction of the new European currency, the euro, in 1999), Germany's concern about its 'national identity' was as much exacerbated as relieved by its appearing, finally, to have become a 'nation state' in 'peace and freedom'.

To seek a common periodisation – to write one history of two Germanies – is to some extent artificial. Although there is increasing interest in this question in united Germany – in part in an attempt to construct a common past for a still less than fully unified society – it is not an exercise in which many academics engaged prior to 1989 [cf. 8].

Some aspects of the intertwined histories of the two Germanies were clearly intimately linked. The mutual interrelations between the two states is the most obvious example: the building of the Wall in 1961 constituted in different ways a common caesura, with effects on the populations on both sides of the Wall, as did the changes following *Ostpolitik*. In a myriad of less obvious ways, neither Germany could quite ignore the other: each constituted for the other both the main enemy and the main competitor, although there were certain asymmetries here. (While West Germany could afford to ignore the GDR's economic performance, East Germany's communist ideals were to some extent subverted by the intense desire to keep up with – even to overtake – the West German economy.) Less obviously, there are many other parallels rooted in often different responses to common challenges, trends and turning points. The formation of different economic and military alliances and developments in superpower relations precipitated a sort of march in tandem, the integration of each state into its respective bloc. Both states responded, in very different ways, to general trends in the international economy (postwar growth, the oil crises of the 1970s, the recession of the 1980s); both were affected by common cultural trends (youth, music, fashion), the emergence of new social movements (feminism, environmentalism, peace) and scientific and technological advances (the growth of mass communication media, transport, computer technology and so on).

Other events and moments of historical significance were more specific to one state or the other. For example the signing of the Helsinki Agreement in 1975, the Biermann affair of 1976 and the church–state accord of 1978 were key events in the GDR but had less impact in the West, which was embroiled in different domestic concerns (such as terrorism – though even this had its links with the GDR). To write an intertwined history is not to deny the separated strands on each side. But even where key historical changes and developments appear quite clearly rooted in one state and not the other – most strikingly perhaps the stability and continuity of the Federal Republic in the 1980s, in contrast to the destabilisation, revolution and collapse of the GDR – the two stories are closely interlinked. After all the collapse of the GDR effectively also, by the successful conclusion of a constitutionally preordained and politically driven unification process, blew the old, safe, affluent and angst-ridden Federal Republic totally out of existence; with

27

the collapse of the Iron Curtain and the incorporation of a quite different state, the Federal Republic of the 1990s could never be the same again.

The history of the two Germanies is thus indeed an intrinsically connected history, even if it is one which is – at least apparently – less simple to write than are most 'national' histories. In the following three chapters particular thematic areas are considered – politics, economy and society, patterns of culture – with respect to the period of division. Chapter 6 then turns to the collapse of the GDR and the nature of unified Germany. We return in Chapter 7 to more general reflections on the intertwined history of the two Germanies.

3 Politics

Academic analyses of democracy and dictatorship in post-Nazi Germany have been extremely closely linked with political and moral evaluations. This is overtly and explicitly the case with Marxist–Leninist critiques of 'bourgeois' democracy and legitimation of the communist regime; it is less obviously but nevertheless often also the case with would-be 'objective' or 'value-neutral' Western analyses of the respective political systems. Curiously the phases of pre-1990 Western academic debate parallel phases in German–German relations, with a softening of tone during the period of détente; there has, however, been a notable repoliticisation of historical debates in the period since unification.

As far as the GDR is concerned, at the height of the Cold War, Western rhetoric focused on 'freedom and democracy' versus 'totalitarian dictatorship'. Western liberal notions of human rights – the right to freedom of speech, freedom of association, freedom of travel – were counterposed to the repression of civil liberties under communism. Needless to say, in East Germany different tones prevailed: official Marxist–Leninist views of the GDR system of 'democratic centralism' emphasised both the alleged historical necessity of the 'dictatorship of the proletariat' (as represented by the vanguard party) in a time of transition, and also enhanced social mobility and egalitarianism as a societal goal in contrast to what were seen as the empty, formal freedoms of capitalism.

Prevalent Western views changed over time. The rejection of the GDR as a 'totalitarian' state, more or less equivalent to Stalin's Russia and Hitler's Germany, came to be modified in the 1970s and 1980s in the light of both changes within the GDR and its relations with the West, and in the context of a changing intellectual climate [for a diatribe against such approaches, see 72].

Although differentiated approaches have been developed, mightily aided by the opening of the East German archives, at the same time highly simplistic, black-and-white, denunciatory views of the GDR have re-emerged with a vengeance in the 1990s among both Eastern and Western scholars [see for example 140, 162; see also my discussion in 1]. There is something of a new polarisation in debates on 'the second German dictatorship'.

Analyses of West German democracy were also affected, to varying degrees, by political evaluations. Marxist–Leninists in the GDR were politically committed to an energetic denunciation of West Germany as the home of Nazis, militarists and imperialists, the epitome of the capitalist system that had brought about Nazism; thus, on this heavily politicised view, a formal change in the political system in the West served merely to mask the basic continuities of socioeconomic structure and personnel. Such rabid denunciations faded in vehemence in the era of *Ostpolitik* and détente (and increasing reliance on West Germany for financial assistance), although few would contend that any serious analyses of the West German political system ever emanated from (or could have been published in) the GDR.

As far as Western analyses of the Federal Republic were concerned, political relevance and political colouring were present but were never quite so anti-empirical in implication. There was an early fascination with the question of political culture: how democratic were West Germans, and was the growing commitment to democracy based purely on pragmatic grounds or was it more principled in nature? [See 33, 48, 182.] As time went by and fears of a resurgence of the past subsided, the question became one of explaining why Bonn democracy was proving to be more stable than Weimar democracy. What, for example, was the role of constitutional provisions as compared with economic success, and how had crucial changes come about?

For those of a more critical persuasion, key questions concerned not the strength but rather the limits of the particular version of 'democracy' operating in the Federal Republic: the restrictions on participatory (as opposed to representative) 'democracy', given the concentration of power with political parties and a range of economic organisations, associations and unions in a system of 'corporatism'; the increasing powers of the state; the very real limits on individual freedom posed by social inequality, poverty or ethnic minority status. The revival of neo-Marxist theories in late-1960s West Germany spawned a variety of 'critiques' of the 'repressive tolerance' of West German democracy, which was not always seen as the 'model state' that some less radical political scientists held it to be.

After unification, left-liberal critiques of West German democracy dwindled; the constitution of the Federal Republic appeared to have been vindicated, to have proved itself the best possible vehicle for 'unification in peace and freedom'; and attention began to be focused on the need for East Germans to 'catch up' with the 'civil society' that had been so successfully established in the West. This more positive evaluation of the Federal Republic, where democracy had been tried and tested and appeared to have been proved 'in the light of history', was the correlate of heightened interest in the functioning of the now defunct GDR.

In pursuing these issues it will be helpful first to outline the formal political systems of the two Germanies.

(i) Political Systems

The constitutions of the two Germanies, when they were created in 1949, were formally rather similar. Both were federal states, with lower and upper houses of parliament, and ceremonial presidents in addition to the political leader (chancellor in the West, prime minister in the East). But even in 1949 the systems were very different in practice.

Free competition among a range of political parties in the West contrasted markedly with the built-in domination in the East of the SED, which increasingly exerted control over the small puppet parties and mass organisations. The GDR was based on a rather different understanding of 'democracy' than that current in the West. In the Marxist–Leninist view the Communist Party had a leading role to play in guiding society through a period of transition, when the old order had not yet been fully disposed of and the masses might still be suffering from the 'false consciousness' instilled in them by capitalist society and its ideologies. The 'dictatorship of the proletariat' would have to be spearheaded by the vanguard party, with no respect for free competition among competing views. The early politics of a common 'antifascist front'

31

(somewhat shallow even in the early occupation period, as the merger between SPD and KPD in April 1946 revealed) gave way from 1948 to a more forceful imposition of communist control over even formally independent organisations. Nevertheless the block parties (NDPD, LDPD, DBD, CDU) and mass organisations – notably the Confederation of Free German Trade Unions (FDGB), the Free German Youth (FDJ), the German-Soviet Friendship Society (DSF), the Democratic Association of German Women (DFD) and the League of Culture (KB) – also had an important role to play as 'transmission belts', upwards as well as downwards, to different sectors of society. Moreover by incorporating large numbers of people within these organisations, over time they helped to secure a system of rule which did not rely solely on the threat or use of overt repression.

As the communists increased their control, excluding former social democrats from the SED and establishing party control over the state, so the formal constitutional structure in the GDR was also altered. The regions, or *Länder*, were abolished in 1952 and the upper house of parliament followed the regions into oblivion in 1958. The role of president was replaced by a collective head of state, the Council of State, on the death of Wilhelm Pieck in 1960. A new constitution in 1968 formally enshrined the leading role of the Marxist–Leninist party; and an amended constitution in 1974 stressed the relationship with the USSR, and emphasised the distinctive identity of the GDR as a separate nation state. There was formally a dual set of hierarchies, but in practice the hierarchy of state (Council of State or *Staatsrat*, Council of Ministers or *Ministerrat*, Parliament or *Volkskammer*, and regional and local representative bodies) was shadowed and dominated by the parallel hierarchy of the SED. This was similarly organised on the principle of democratic centralism, with a hierarchy of power and authority running down from the Politburo through the Central Committee, the national party conferences and congresses and the regional and local party organisations, to the 'basic organisations', workplace and residentially based cells.

The 1949 Basic Law of the Federal Republic was designed with acute regard for the failure of Germany's previous attempt at democracy in the Weimar Republic. Intended safeguards against a repeat performance included a combination of proportional representation with 'first-past-the-post' directly elected constituency

MPs; a (subsequently introduced) electoral hurdle, such that small parties which failed to gain 5 per cent of the national vote (or a directly elected MP) would not gain national representation and create difficulties for viable coalition formation; a more purely ceremonial role for the president, who was to be elected by an electoral college rather than mass popular vote; and a device known as the 'constructive vote of no confidence', intended to ensure that chancellors could not be ousted without a nominated successor who could command parliamentary support, failing which a national election would be held. Political parties were to contribute to forming the political will of the people, and there were detailed regulations on their funding, organisation and activities. Parties which did not uphold the 'free-democratic' basic tenets of the constitution could be banned – this was applied to the right-wing Socialist Reich Party (SRP) in 1952 and the Communist Party of Germany (KPD) in 1956 (the latter was permitted to refound itself as the DKP in 1968). A constitutional court in Karlsruhe had the power to adjudicate on constitutional issues.

One particular feature of the Federal Republic – as of course its name implies – is the federal system. Germany had a long history of regional particularism, dating from its origins in the decentralised medieval Holy Roman Empire (which came to an end in 1806), and preserved through the Confederation of 1815–66, the unified Imperial Germany of 1871–1918 and the succeeding Weimar Republic, which ended with Hitler's accession to power in 1933. Hitler of course sought to abolish the autonomy of the regions. But even in Imperial and Weimar Germany the federal system was somewhat out of balance due to the dominance of one state: Prussia. With the effective partition and dismemberment of this state in 1945, followed by its formal abolition in 1947, the federalism of the Federal Republic of Germany differed somewhat from its pre-Nazi predecessors. States such as Bavaria (expanded from its medieval core in 'old Bavaria' by Napoleon, and inventing a host of 'traditions' in the nineteenth century) and the proud, formerly independent Hanse town of Hamburg, had long histories and well-defined profiles. Others were, however, either more recent amalgamations (Baden-Württemberg) or, as in the case of North-Rhine Westphalia, a quite new creation. West Berlin retained a distinctive status as a part of a city formally still under four-power control, but in practice, so far as possible, incorporated as a functioning part of the federal system. The constituent states of the Federal Republic remained important centres of regional government, and had a powerful input into national political processes through the upper house of parliament, the Bundesrat. They also, from the 1970s, began to develop new modes of cooperation and equalisation of conditions among themselves. The federal system of West Germany appeared to have resolved the problem of harmonising a relatively high degree of regional particularism in a traditionally decentralised country with the demands on central government in an advanced industrial state. The decentralisation of the Federal Republic was to some extent underlined by the loss of the former capital, Berlin. The 'provisional' capital of the new rump state, Bonn, was modest and unpretentious – merely a 'small town in Germany' – and governmental functions were physically separated from the financial centre of Frankfurt and the multiplicity of cultural centres across the country.

The Basic Law was sufficiently flexible to develop, along with the development of the Federal Republic, without a fundamentally new constitution being required. Critics suggested that certain amendments (such as the emergency legislation of the 1960s) fundamentally altered the balance of the constitution and rendered it less democratic. Others praised the Basic Law as providing the foundation for the stability of West German democracy – and the flexibility to incorporate the newly reconstituted *Länder* of East Germany as a means of unification in 1990. Certainly the Basic Law provided a framework for a more successful and democratic state than in the past, although in practice the success of West German democracy had a lot to do with factors other than formal constitutional provisions, not least economic success. But other changes, too, including the sheer passage of time, the passing of generations and the development of new structures and processes, increasingly made West Germany appear less like the rump of a severed nation, the threatening remnants of a defeated Nazi past, and increasingly, like a 'normal' Western democracy, an acceptable variant of typical political patterns, and one which many Western observers felt was worth analysing and in some respects even emulating.

To understand fully the political dynamics of the two Germanies it is inadequate to remain at the level of formal analysis of systems. We must consider the development and actual functioning of political life over time.

(ii) Political Developments in West Germany

There were major changes, first of all, in the parties which represented important pillars of West German democracy. In the early years – from the foundation or refoundation of parties in the occupation period to the early 1950s – the party system looked rather similar to that of the Weimar Republic: there was a multiplicity of parties, some representing very specific groups (such as the refugees and expellees), while others were more broadly based. It was not at all clear that problems of stable coalition formation would not plague Bonn democracy in the manner of the Weimar Republic. [For a variety of introductions to the development of West German democracy see for example 5, 15, 58, 98, 145, 154, 180; a rather more blatantly biased account may be found in 7; for a useful collection of documents in translation see 167.]

In the course of the 1950s two major changes took place. First, the CDU – in the light of the economic miracle, as well as the effective pardon granted to former Nazis who were not guilty of war crimes – succeeded in absorbing the small right-wing parties and became a relatively broad-based conservative 'people's party' (*Volkspartei*), including both Catholics and, to a lesser extent, Protestants. Secondly, in the light of the CDU's success there was a dramatic transformation of the character of the SPD. At the 1959 Bad Godesberg conference the social democrats decided to renounce their Marxist rhetoric and adopt a more moderate image, seeking to become a similar form of catch-all party with broad appeal. The party system developed into a choice between two major parties, both committed to the social market economy and the continuance of capitalism, with the small liberal party, the FDP, holding the balance of power. Given the convergence between the CDU and SPD – although major differences remained, particularly over foreign policy – some analysts characterised West German democracy by the early 1960s in terms of a 'vanishing opposition' [101]. Under the Grand Coalition of 1966–69 between the SPD and the CDU, parliamentary opposition was to disappear almost entirely.

35

This 'vanishing' of parliamentary opposition was far from complete: major differences between the SPD and CDU emerged over the issue of relations with East Germany (*Ostpolitik*) under Willy Brandt's new social–liberal government from 1969. But the previous period of convergence was accompanied by changes at the margins of establishment politics. On the left, the students' movement fed into the formation of an 'extraparliamentary opposition' (*Ausserparlamentarische Opposition*, or APO) and into the explosion of radical ideas and activities in 1968. On the right, the minor economic recession of the mid 1960s boosted support for the neo-Nazi NPD, which had certain successes in *Land* elections in the late 1960s. Neither of these movements as such was long-lived: the NPD soon faded, having failed to make an impact at the national level, while the students' movement splintered and diversified into a range of groups and orientations in the 1970s. Nevertheless the development of more extremist politics was of longer-term significance. Left-wing initiatives contributed to the rise of a range of social movements, pressure groups and 'citizens' initiative groups' in the course of the 1970s, as well as the formation of 'Alternative List' parties. The most significant new party to emerge from these developments was the Greens. Their concern with environmental issues and the potential political threat they posed, particularly to the voting base of the SPD, ensured that certain topics had to rise higher on the explicit agenda of the major parties.

After the swing to a conservative–liberal coalition in 1982 the party system of the Federal Republic appeared to be in a state of flux again. The results of *Land* elections seemed to indicate a rising proportion of voters who were not firmly committed to any of the established parties, and who were to a degree disaffected with the whole voting system itself. Voter volatility and disaffection gave particular cause for concern in connection with relatively high regional votes for two new right-wing parties, capitalising on resentment against foreign workers in Germany; the Republicans (*Republikaner*) and the German People's Union (*Deutsche Volksunion* or DVU). These trends were, however, dramatically affected by the extraordinary changes in German political life associated with the collapse of the GDR and the unification of Germany. In the first all-German elections of December 1990 the CDU rode to victory under the 'unification chancellor', Helmut Kohl. The social democrats – whose rather more realistic warnings about the economic consequences of unification did not appear to be accompanied by sufficient political enthusiasm for the project – lost votes, while the environmentalist concerns of the Greens were largely incorporated into mainstream policies.

On one view, West German democracy developed from being largely representative – as intended by the Allies, who did not fully trust the judgements of the German people in view of their recent history – to being more participatory. The high electoral turnouts of the 1950s and early 1960s were interpreted by some American political scientists as evidence of a 'subject' rather than a 'citizen' mentality: doing one's duty to the authoritarian state. But the high turnout in the 1972 election was clearly evidence of wide public interest in the issue of *Ostpolitik* (and support for Brandt's policies). And the rise of all manner of pressure groups at local and national level in the 1970s and 1980s also indicated a greater desire on the part of many citizens to participate in the processes of policy formation and decision making.

This may have been a salutary development from the point of view of popular political culture, even though political activists clearly remained only a small minority of the population. But it is less clear whether the locus of power in the West German state really shifted significantly. The degree to which citizen participation influenced policy making on different issues (ranging from defence strategies to waste disposal) is an open question. Moreover there are other relevant aspects of West German democracy to consider.

Some analysts focus heavily on the nature – in terms of class, gender and religion – of those individuals who are elected as 'representatives of the people'. Such analysis relatively easily points to the underrepresentation of women, of people from disadvantaged socioeconomic backgrounds and of ethnic minorities in national politics. In conjunction with other powerful groups – such as the judiciary and the civil servants who advise policy makers – it is relatively easy to identify what may be called (in the American sociologist C. Wright Mills' phrase) a set of 'power elites'. Others have argued that the social backgrounds and personal attributes of the national legislators are, for a variety of reasons, to a degree, irrelevant.

For one thing, in a federal state the locus of political decision making is more decentralised and a range of subsidiary bodies are involved in policy processes. For another, and only partly related to this, a form of 'corporatism' developed in the Federal Republic (based on a fairly long historical tradition of interest group participation in policy formation). Major interest groups – the employers' federation, representatives of the farming lobby, trade unionists – came together to work out the details of acceptable policy compromises before any draft legislation was put to parliament for final, almost purely formal, approval. Radicals, seeing the greater resources and power of capital rather than labour in this process, criticised what was seen as a less than democratic process of policy making behind the scenes, which in any event completely excluded certain disadvantaged groups with no powerful lobby to act on their behalf. Other political scientists, however, praised this system as a means of ensuring that proposed policies were workable and acceptable to all parties affected [cf the discussions in 33, 48].

Clearly West German democracy was characterised by certain restrictions in practice; and equally it was not without its scandals and corruption, as demonstrated by the bribery and intrigues surrounding the parliamentary debates on *Ostpolitik* in the early 1970s and the 'Flick affair' (named after the Flick conglomerate) of the 1980s, in which illicit practices in tax evasion and the 'laundering' of corporate donations to party funds were revealed. Similarly there were good grounds for radicals to be wary of the increased powers of the state and the restrictions on personal freedom of speech and association that were involved in the 'Decree Concerning Radicals' (*Radikalenerlaß*) of 1972, and the measures taken to deal with the terrorist wave of the later 1970s [for one heated contribution to these debates see for example 32]. And there was some basis for the charge that policy differences between the Conservative and Social Democratic Parties were relatively minor, consisting more in differences of emphasis with respect to levels of taxation and welfare expenditure, for example, than in any fundamental difference of political principle. By the 1980s both major parties were seeking wide appeal as moderate managers of the capitalist state, with the FDP having little difficulty in swinging its allegiance from one to the other when it suited it so to do.

But at the same time the democracy of the Federal Republic of Germany had proved, over four decades, to be a resilient and relatively flexible system. The federal structure appeared to have operated well, with a degree of regional autonomy allowing space for the different traditions and characters of the *Länder*, while degrees of cooperation enhanced resources for some and ensured more effective implementation of policies in other areas. While there were minority currents of political extremism, with the passage of generations a higher proportion of West Germans had become committed democrats. And, despite the Federal Republic's constitutionally enshrined status as a 'provisional' state, by the 1980s the Federal Republic of Germany could command, in left–liberal quarters, a certain 'patriotism of the constitution' (*Verfassungspatriotismus*) alongside a commitment to European integration and 'post-nationalism', which at least for some West Germans seemed an acceptable replacement for the discredited and difficult heritage of German nationalism.

(iii) Political Developments in the GDR

Not least in importance in affecting the nature and development of the GDR was the Soviet Union. The USSR was the creator of the East German communist state, and was also a major player in the manner of its end. Along the way it intervened in countless ways to affect the course of development, and even (both in the early years and again at the end) to decide whether the GDR should continue to exist at all. To view the GDR as a self-contained system is to ignore this central determinant of its existence. Bearing this external parameter in mind, there nevertheless remain significant questions about the domestic political configuration of the GDR [for a fuller discussion see 59].

The main feature of the GDR, striking to every observer, whether Eastern or Western, was the fact that it had to rely on the effective imprisonment of its population. The 'Iron Curtain' of the long fortified border between East and West Germany, and from 1961 the Berlin Wall, seemed to stand as visible proof of the GDR's political bankruptcy, its ultimate reliance on physical force as a means of ensuring stability. Add to the border guards the omnipresence of Soviet troops, the extensive network of military forces, the people's police, the workers' militia groups and – last but certainly by no means least – the State Security Police, or Stasi, and it seemed to some observers quite clear that the GDR was essentially built on simple repression.

39

In the aftermath of the 1989 revolution the extent of this repression became ever more clear. The role of the Stasi in particular began to be revealed in its full extent [see for some examples 4, 11, 17, 22, 31, 40, 56, 59, 62, 65, 139]. It seemed that files had been kept on around three quarters of the adult population of the GDR. A vast network of informers, informal collaborators and people in a wide range of social positions had not only kept the information service well abreast of developments, but also assisted in the task of seeking to destroy any kernel of potential opposition to the regime. There are debates about the precise extent and meaning of collaboration with the Stasi, but few erstwhile informers survived the *Wende* unscathed (the prime minister of *Land* Brandenburg, Manfred Stolpe, being a notable exception). Whether the Stasi merely operated (as it proclaimed) as the 'sword and shield of the party', or (as those party supporters seeking a degree of exoneration preferred) as a 'state within a state', or whether it performed a more vital role as the essential brain centre and nervous system of the GDR, its malign and duplicitous role is undeniable.

Alongside this repression went the ultimate and, from 1968, constitutionally enshrined power of the Marxist–Leninist party, the SED. This, with its puppet parties and mass organisations, clearly dominated the state and was the guardian and articulator of official ideology, the definer of orthodoxy, heterodoxy and heresy. At least in principle the SED and its allied organisations sought, in a relatively paternalistic if always paranoid fashion, to improve the lot of 'the people' – at least in the long term, even if this meant going against expressed wishes and suppressing democratic debate in the immediate present. Slightly more complex were the relations between the SED state and the one remaining relatively independent social institution in the GDR, the churches. The highly ambivalent tightrope along which the churches walked contributed both to the stability and the ultimate destabilisation of the GDR [for an example of by now wide-ranging discussions – or more usually indictments – of the role of the churches in German see for example 16; for less partisan discussions in English see 59, 68].

There were of course changes in the system over time. During the 1950s political repression and terror was much more evident than in later decades (at least until the return to open use of force

40

from late 1987 onwards). Following the rapid suppression of the June Uprising of 1953, when the West opted for international stability over intervention on behalf of the East German people, most ordinary people in the GDR confined themselves to a form of grumbling conformity [but cf. 73 and 114]. Gradually other aspects of the political system began to function more smoothly. In the 1960s, with an assured labour supply after the building of the Wall and a focus on scientific and technical expertise, new career opportunities were opened up in the GDR. Professional groups, as well as those who had benefited from the social mobility fostered by Ulbricht, began to feel they had a stake in the system. It was for this period that Peter-Christian Ludz designed the concept of 'consultative authoritarianism' [see 124, 125, 126]. In the 1970s, when Honecker announced the 'unity of social and economic policy' and – at least initially – relaxed controls on cultural production, many people also felt that the GDR was a place in which one could work for change in a more positive direction. Such views were given sustenance by the outcome of *Ostpolitik*, the eased communications with the West following the Basic Treaty of 1972, the GDR's full membership of the United Nations in 1973 and its participation in the Helsinki process, including the promise to respect human rights. There were however always warning signs – symbolised for example by the enforced expatriation of Wolf Biermann and the self-burning of Pastor Brüsewitz in 1976 – and it was, paradoxically, in the time of apparently greater lenience and openness in the 1970s and 1980s that the Stasi itself mushroomed exponentially in size. But it was only in the late 1980s, when developments such as the unofficial peace initiatives and human rights movements seemed to be snowballing out of the control of the state, that repression again became apparent on a scale commensurate with the use of force in the early 1950s.

How important was force as a factor in the stability of the GDR? Do the undoubtedly repressive features of the East German dictatorship add up to a simple description – and effective dismissal – of the GDR as 'totalitarian'? The concept of totalitarianism had great popularity in the 1950s, and after a period in some disgrace it reappeared in political science writings in the late 1970s and 1980s. Since unification it has enjoyed an extraordinary renaissance [see for example Schroeder, and Schroeder and Staadt, in 162]. There are however several problems with this concept.

41

For one thing, even as a purely typological, classificatory device it has shortcomings. Even among those who agree that they want to call the GDR a totalitarian state, there is still no generally accepted operationalisation of the concept. (Nor, it should be noted, was there in its heyday in the 1950s: the definitions by Hannah Arendt, and Friedrich and Brzezinski were very different from each other in emphasis.) Some use it simply as shorthand for repression; others link it to an alleged 'de-differentiation of spheres'; others link it to the concept of 'political religion'.

But those who employ the concept claim that it goes beyond mere classification and suggest that it is also explanatory. Here, too, there are difficulties. These relate in part to the difficulty of capturing changes over time (as noted above), although some analysts make gestures towards escaping a tendency to static analysis. More problematically the emphasis on repression does not actually help very much in explaining patterns of stability and change over time; thus, for example, on this model it is difficult to explain why the GDR collapsed in 1989 at precisely the moment when its repressive apparatus was at its largest and most sophisticated. It also misses a great deal when the focus is not on the apparatus of repression, but rather on the variety of ways in which 'state' and 'society' interacted. The GDR was not simply, and at all times, only sustained against the will of members of the populace by the massive threat or use of force.

By focusing so heavily on certain aspects of political life the concept of totalitarianism obscures or deflects attention from other important features of the system in operation. Although force may have been the bottom line, the reality is somewhat more complex.

For one thing there is the issue of space for freedom of debate, lack of ideological commitment, the articulation of dissenting views. Ulbricht's early attempts at total ideological indoctrination were eventually relaxed (and were in any event unrealisable). Under Honecker, in some ways it was possible to live without adhering strictly to the official world view. The effective toleration of the church, the acceptance that religion would not wither away and that Christians and Marxists should 'work hand in hand' to build a better society represented official acceptance of an – albeit very limited – ideological pluralism in the GDR.

There were also important state-sustaining currents. Despite the fact that the enhanced importance of the technical intelligentsia in the 1960s led Ludz to perceive the incipient rise of a 'counter-elite' [124; but see 10], most functional elites were characterised by a high degree of conformity. In a rather different way, much the same can be said of the cultural intelligentsia. Those who were too critical or politically uncomfortable were readily exiled or persuaded to leave for the West; the others, whether pro-regime hacks or semi-critical voices, led relatively privileged lives, with frequent trips to the West and access to Western currency, and effectively made compromises with the regime (including a degree of self-censorship) in order to continue their work.

Such compromises were characteristic of far wider and less privileged sections of the populace too. The fact that as many as one in five of the adult population were prepared to join the SED says something too about the degree of political conformity. The more or less saturation membership of the trade union organisation (the FDGB) and the substantial participation in the youth organisations (the Thälmann Pioneers and the FDJ) are indicative not only of the way in which the state 'drenched' society, but also of the ways in which rising generations were in part constituted by and through their participation in such organisations. It may be hard for outsiders (both literal and political) to grasp, but the weight of evidence on popular opinion from perhaps the early 1970s to the mid 1980s suggests that a majority of those younger GDR citizens who were born and bred in this state simply accepted its parameters as 'the way things are'. It was only in the Gorbachev era, in the context of growing challenges to Honecker's rule, that this picture changed.

This brings us to the issue of political dissent [on opposition see generally 143]. What was surprising about the regime's final collapse was both the sudden emergence of mass civil courage and the speed of the capitulation of the authorities in the face of popular protest. Regime stability is as much to be explained by *lack* of effective opposition as it is by the threat or use of force (in dictatorships) or the active support of the populace (in democracies). The GDR was not without its moments of active opposition. In June 1953 it experienced the first popular uprising in Eastern Europe (followed in later years by splutterings of revolt in Hungary, Poland and Czechoslovakia). This largely spontaneous expression of protest originated in domestic socioeconomic policies and spread into more general political demands; but it was largely lacking in

43

leadership, organisation and strategy, as well as support from the West, and – despite the notable lack of preparedness on the part of the East German security and repressive forces – it was relatively easily suppressed. In 1968, outward appearances to the contrary, there was significant discontent within the GDR following the suppression by Warsaw Pact troops of the 'Prague Spring' in Czechoslovakia. Again, however, these individual protests – which had far less anchorage in domestic issues – were relatively easily suppressed by a now much larger and more efficient security apparatus. For much of the 1960s and 1970s the handful of East German intellectual dissidents remained essentially voices crying in the wilderness, easily isolated or exiled to the West. It was only in the late 1970s and 1980s that a tiny minority of political activists seeking reform within the GDR began to form organised groups and networks, initially under the protective wing of the churches after the 1978 agreement. And it was only in the dramatically changed circumstances of summer and autumn 1989 that wider numbers began to emerge as a significant force on the political stage, whether seeking 'exit' or 'voice'.

Simply adducing the repressive powers of the dictatorship does little to illuminate the complexity of these developments, nor to explain (let alone understand) the levels of general support and accommodation. On closer inspection it turns out that the concept of totalitarianism is suited less to the purpose of academic explanation than to that of denunciation. While accepting the need, particularly among former victims of repressive regimes, to vent their emotions on a hated state by adopting as a label what is essentially a term of abuse, one can nevertheless point to the shortcomings of seeking to adapt this term of abuse to the purposes of scholarly analysis.

Given the implicit and sometimes explicit comparisons of communist and Nazi rule, it may at this point be worth raising the concept of 'polycracy', which has by and large replaced totalitarianism as a concept for analysing the power structure of the Third Reich. Does this help us along any further? Clearly the GDR was a system capable of self-reproduction and development, rather than being an expansionist, destructive and ultimately self-destructive system, as was the Third Reich. There was a vast gulf between the relatively smooth organisation of politics in the GDR and the infinitely more chaotic, multicentred political processes obtaining in the

Third Reich. And not only was the whole East German system more streamlined; the use of physical terror by the Stasi (with its very extensive network of informers) was both smaller in scale and more subtle in practice than that of the openly brutal Gestapo.

Finally the role of the leader in the GDR – although puffed up in a typical communist leadership cult – was actually very much less important in seeking to obtain real popular support for or acquiescence in the regime, in contrast to the charismatic role of Adolf Hitler in holding together the competitive, overlapping and centrifugal forces of the Third Reich. Thus whatever shared dislike there may be of the two successive dictatorships, there seems little sense in seeking to adopt an analytic concept for the GDR which derives from the very different workings of Hitler's state.

The differences between the GDR and the Third Reich are numerous, and adequate exploration would require much more space than is available here. There are clearly both advantages and difficulties in attempting to develop concepts for the purpose of historical comparison. The notion of totalitarianism is perhaps more misleading than helpful with respect to both the Nazi and the SED dictatorships. Polycracy does not appear helpful with respect to the communist dictatorship of the GDR. Some historians are now trying to develop new concepts to capture the distinctive characteristics of 'modern' dictatorships – from Stalin to Hitler – none of which are uncontentious. In part the problem lies in trying to develop a holistic concept to embrace and account for the whole.

A more useful approach would be to reject the attempt to encompass the whole (particularly when this extends over forty years of change) and to adopt instead a set of analytically separable concepts which refer to more specific areas and are not tied together in a global bundle. Particular combinations of factors and historical configurations, under different circumstances, could then be explored, allowing for accuracy with respect to any one case and also comparisons and contrasts with other cases. Some of the more interesting narrative histories of the GDR have in fact attempted to do this, although there has not so far been any successful attempt at the systematisation and broader application of such an approach.

To do this effectively would require further research into certain key aspects of East German politics. Particularly important subjects of investigation include: the development and internal dynamics of the SED itself, and the actual structures of decision making; the political orientations and roles of key elite groups; the development of dissenting views and organisations, particularly in respect of the proliferation of grass-roots dissent in the 1980s; and the developments among different social groups in a changing socio-economic, cultural and international context.

4 Economy and Society

Differences in wealth and economic performance between East and West Germany were perhaps the most striking feature to outside observers when the Wall came down. While the success of the West German economy was scarcely in doubt, simplistic platitudes about communism disguise a somewhat more complex picture when examined in detail [see generally 39, 41, 90, 113, 115, 122, 144, 155, 169].

There were clearly differences in 1945 between the socioeconomic profiles of the areas of Germany which were to become the Federal Republic and the GDR respectively. West Germany contained the major industrial area of the Ruhr, as well as the coal-rich Saar basin (the Saar only formally became a *Land* of the Federal Republic after a plebiscite in 1957), and was on the whole more densely populated than the areas of East Germany. Sparseness of population was one reason why the Soviet zone in fact covered a relatively large land area, since zones of occupation were to have more or less comparable population sizes (with the exception of the French zone, carved out of the British and American zones, which had been agreed earlier). East German natural resources were fewer, having to rely on the inferior brown coal (lignite) for energy, for example. But on the other hand there were also major industrial centres in the southern areas of what became the GDR, while West Germany too had large areas of forest and heathland not used for agricultural production. Moreover what became the GDR had on the whole suffered less bomb damage in the war than had the western areas of Germany. So the initial differences in economic profile and potential were not so great.

But already in 1945 major changes were instigated. With the land reform in the Soviet zone and subsequent policies – effected at intervals over the next two decades – of nationalisation and

47

collectivisation, there was what amounted to a revolution in socio-economic structure. Although in the course of the 1970s and 1980s the GDR was generally proclaimed to be the most productive state in the Soviet bloc, following its collapse in 1990 the true extent of economic instability and spiralling decline was revealed. The question then arises as to whether the eventual collapse was endemic to a centrally planned communist economy in principle, or whether the mounting economic crises which were becoming increasingly evident in the 1980s were not contingent on poor decisions taken by Honecker's leadership team in the context of world recession following the oil crises of 1973 and 1979, accompanied by a growing mini-Cold War in the Reagan era.

By contrast it has often been remarked that West Germany, having lost the war, won the peace. Or, in another famous characterisation, despite being a 'political dwarf', post-Nazi West Germany was able to become an 'economic giant'. The 'economic miracle' of the first decade or so of the Federal Republic's history and the subsequent powerful performance of the West German economy have prompted many analysts to search for the secret of German success. Does it lie in some aspect of West German industrial relations, its renowned (or supposed) social partnership and relatively trouble-free strike record? Does it lie in the financial management of West Germany, with a fear of inflation harking back to the catastrophe of 1923, with highly restricted consumer credit and close control of the economy by an independent central bank? How important was early massive American investment through the Marshall Plan, and the subsequent general regeneration of the West European economy?

While the very real divergences between the economies of the two Germanies were acutely visible – and had major consequences for the rapid unification of the two once the Wall had fallen – there is, paradoxically, another set of questions which have to do not with divergence but with the arguable convergence of the two societies. Clearly the differences between centralised communist and market capitalist states and their patterns of economic and social policy were major. But some analysts have claimed to discern a 'convergence' of all industrial societies, whatever their overt political differences. On this view the problems of managing large-scale, complex industrial societies threw up comparable organisational patterns: for example, given the importance of the

48

managerial class, it made little real difference whether ownership was in the hands of a number of largely anonymous shareholders or in the hands of the state in the name of the people; expert technocrats and bureaucrats supposedly came to have comparable positions of influence, irrespective of the formal differences between political systems; the proportion of manual and non-manual workers, and the proportion of workers in industry, agriculture and the service sector, supposedly also changed at comparable rates.

(i) Economic Structures and Development

One striking aspect of West German economic development is a certain continuity with earlier trends. Although the Western Allies wanted the Federal Republic to mark a clear break with the past, this was less the case in the economic arena than in the political. In the occupation period the Americans (and, under American pressure, the British) even intervened to prevent the passage of measures permitting the socialisation of key areas of the economy in different *Länder*, protecting private ownership of the means of production against more radical approaches favoured at that time by many Germans. In reaction against the recent Nazi past, state guidance of the economy was to be eased under the neoliberal concept of a 'social market economy'; this meant that while there was to be as much of a free market as possible there was still to be a role for state interference, both to ensure the conditions for rendering capitalist enterprise profitable, and to provide a social welfare safety net for those who were victims of the market [144]. And although the Allies were concerned to achieve a deconcentration and decartelisation of German industry, even after the (belated) passage of a decartelisation law in 1957 there were sufficient loopholes for previous patterns to continue. In both structure and to a large extent personnel, the postwar West German economy was characterised more by continuity than radical change. It was only in the course of the 1960s that the attitudes at least of a new generation of 'managers' (the word was appropriated in German) began to be Americanised [14]. Many distinctive practices in West German industrial relations, such as works' councils and codetermination, in fact had their origins in the Weimar Republic, while

49

corporatist approaches in general stretched back to Bismarck's era.

In the Federal Republic, patterns of industrial relations and state–business links developed which were rather different from those in other West European capitalist economies. In 1951 a measure of 'codetermination' (*Mitbestimmung*) was introduced in enterprises with over 1000 employees in the iron and steel industry, allowing representatives of the workforce a say in management decisions, including manpower planning – although management retained the chair's casting vote. The Codetermination Law (*Mitbestimmungsgesetz*) of 1976 stipulated that all limited companies with over 2000 employees should introduce codetermination and joint decision making. In 1952 Works Councils for joint discussion of matters internal to an industry were established; the principle was extended in the Works Constitution Act of 1972. These measures provided the basis for the claim that German industrial relations were peculiarly harmonious, characterised by a 'social partnership'. Although West German workers were indeed less strike-prone than their British counterparts (for a variety of reasons, including rapidly rising standards of living and an unwillingness to rock the economic boat), much of the legislation was introduced against considerable opposition on the part of the employers – who even challenged the 1976 legislation, although the Constitutional Court finally overruled their appeal in 1979 – and accompanied by some disappointment on the part of the unions [see 13].

Not all features of West German industrial relations were built on earlier traditions; some represented a degree of learning from earlier mistakes. Rejecting the religious and ideological fragmentation of the trade unions in Imperial Germany and the Weimar Republic, a streamlined and simplified structure of politically neutral 'industrial unions' was adopted. This meant that there was only one union per industry, thus avoiding rivalry between competing unions, simplifying the bargaining process with employers (who could not divide and rule) and strengthening the union position in negotiations over collective agreements on wages and conditions. (This also differed, of course, from the British heritage of a multiplicity of fragmented unions politically tied to the Labour Party – which was founded, historically, as the parliamentary wing of the labour movement.) The seventeen industrial unions in West Germany – of which the largest was I. G. Metall – together formed the German Trade Union Federation, the DGB. The DGB, the employers' Federation of German Industry and the state together took some responsibility for joint decision making in what was known as a form of 'corporatism', seeking to circumvent damaging conflicts of interests by prior negotiation and compromise. This took a distinctive form during the period of 'Concerted Action' from 1967 to 1977 (terminating when the unions withdrew as a result of tension over the employers' challenge to the extension of codetermination), but was characteristic of many decision-making processes over a much longer period, including behind-the-scenes negotiations between interest groups prior to parliamentary legislation.

There were of course changes over time in the structure and performance of the West German economy, within the broad limits of the much-vaunted 'social market' framework. The neo-liberalism of the 1950s and the first half of the 1960s gave way to a neo-Keynesianism in the late 1960s, with – particularly under the social democratic/liberal government in the early 1970s – considerable energy devoted to the attempted state-steering of the economy. Under the conditions of world recession following the oil crisis of 1973, this gave way to a more reactive pattern of crisis management. Following the return to conservative government after 1982, neo-liberal economic ideas again replaced Keynesianism. But with the FDP holding the balance of power as an almost permanent coalition partner there was less radical changing of economic policies between governments in West Germany than there was in Britain: there was neither, on the one hand, extensive nationalisation under social democratic governments, nor, on the other, the passion for privatisation and extensive rejection of state support for essential public services (such as the railway network) or energy supplies (such as coal) under conservative German governments as there was in Britain under Mrs Thatcher.

The economic structure of East Germany was of course very different. The land reform of autumn 1945 effectively abolished large estates, and with them the class of the Prussian *Junkers*; the subsequent collectivisation of agriculture, in two major waves (1952 and 1960), was largely complete by the beginning of the 1960s and put a comparable end to an independent peasantry. Collectivisation measures were at first detrimental to agricultural

51

production, and contributed both to increased numbers of refugees and to the political difficulties of 1953 and 1961 (the June Uprising and the building of the Wall). But matters improved. Agricultural specialisation – such as fruit farming – in large collectives, with the associated benefits of scale, was developed in the 1970s and 1980s. At the same time the cultivation of small allotments was encouraged to supplement supplies of fresh produce. While the GDR needed to import grain for animal foodstuffs, East Germany became largely self-sufficient as far as feeding her human population was concerned (if at a rather basic level, with little choice of fresh fruits and vegetables).

The nationalisation of finance and industry in the GDR and the squeezing of an ever-diminishing private sector led ultimately to what some commentators have called a form of 'state capitalism'. Under a system of central planning the state determined levels and types of productive output, often with little regard for consumer interests. In the 1950s quantity was emphasised at the expense of quality and even demand; heavy industry (and the demands of remilitarisation) took precedence over the production of consumer durables. The limits of state exploitation of workers' productivity were revealed in the 1953 uprising, but dislocations in supply and the inadequacies of central planning led to continuing difficulties. A certain measure of decentralisation was introduced in the New Economic System of 1963–70, which seemed to promise a more flexible system, introducing profit incentives and greater decision-making powers at intermediate levels. This experiment was, however, never given sufficient time for a real trial: in the aftermath of the Czech 'Prague Spring' of 1968 it was terminated for largely political rather than economic reasons. In the 1970s and 1980s central control of the economy was combined with (from the late 1970s) increased centralisation at lower levels, in large combines (*Kombinate*). Honecker's emphasis on consumer satisfaction was combined with an almost obsessive desire to lead the Soviet world in computer technology; from the late 1970s – and ever more visibly from the early 1980s – the GDR economy developed spiralling debts (and an increasing financial reliance on assistance from the conservative government of the Federal Republic in the unlikely person of Franz Josef Strauß of the CSU). Warnings from those few economic experts within the GDR who knew the true figures were not heeded, as the simultaneous pursuit of economic growth and consumer satisfaction brought increasingly obvious ecological and financial disasters in their wake, with the eventual political consequences of 1989–90 [cf. 39]. What of the role of the workers in the 'workers' and peasants' state'? All workers belonged to the single trade union organisation, the League of Free German Trade Unions (FDGB), which has generally been represented as less a body representing workers' interests than a mouthpiece of the ruling SED. Nevertheless this offered notable benefits for its membership (around 100 per cent of the workforce) in the form of organised holidays as well as day-to-day intervention in disputes relating to working conditions, premiums, wage rates and the like. Furthermore it has been argued that workers to some extent exercised a veto power over the kinds of policy the SED was able to effect [113]. But the GDR, although it valued 'the working class' very highly in ideology, was in reality far from being a workers' paradise in which – according to Marx's theory – 'alienation' had been overcome. There is little evidence to suggest that people *felt* any less 'alienated' when undertaking long, boring hours of tedious and unpleasant shift-work in a 'peoples' own factory' (*Volkseigener Betrieb*, or VEB) than they did in a West German capitalist factory where the working conditions, pay, hours and holiday entitlement were very much better. Nevertheless, although recognising these material differentials, many East German workers at the same time valued their sense of security of employment.

Clearly, given the different ideologies upon which the two Germanies were based, there were very marked differences in their economic structures. There were also very visible differences in their patterns of economic development and performance.

West Germany early benefited from the receipt of Marshall Aid and the associated climate of confidence. The West German economy was able to reap benefits too from the Korean War, and from the influx of skilled, mobile labour from the East in the 1950s. The rapid economic take-off became known as the 'economic miracle'. Growth rates in the 1950s averaged around 8 per cent, with bumper years in 1951 (10.4 per cent) and 1955 (12 per cent) and only lulling somewhat in 1957 and 1958 (5.7 per cent and 3.7 per cent respectively). This period of early rapid expansion led into a longer-term pattern of sustained performance, with slight recessions in 1966–67, 1974–75 and 1981–82.

The enviable performance of the West German economy was characterised by unique relations between banks and industry, restricted consumer credit, encouragement for investment, and low inflation and unemployment rates compared with other West European economies.

West Germany's increasingly powerful economy came to play a distinctive role in processes of European integration, first in the European Coal and Steel Community (ECSC) and then, as a founder member of the EEC and signatory to the Treaty of Rome in 1957, in the broader European Community (EC). As a trading nation, West Germany's major trading partners were the EC countries. While West Germany was a major contributor to the EC budget there were certain political benefits to be gained from her role. In particular a stress on European integration both emphasised West Germany's willingness to cooperate rather than appear threatening and played some role – although one which is difficult to define or quantify with any precision – in forging a new sense of identity for West Germans in the period after the defeat of the Third Reich. By the close of the 1980s, in any event, the West German economy and role in Europe were a focus of widespread admiration as well as analysis.

The East German economy, by contrast, had to run something of an obstacle course and it is perhaps remarkable that its performance was not infinitely worse. Ravaged by the Soviets' early reparations policy, ripped from its natural links to the West, reorientated towards the less developed economies of the Comecon bloc, radically restructured and experiencing a whole series of dislocations and difficulties, the East German economy achieved something of its own miracle in sustaining a modest level of growth. Accurate figures are still difficult to calculate, but the average rate of growth of the East German economy in the 1960s and 1970s was probably in the order of 3 per cent a year, with increasing economic difficulties and a less creditable performance in the 1980s. For all its problems the GDR economy attained and surpassed the performance of the Soviet economy, and under Honecker began to satisfy a rather basic level of consumer demand for goods such as fridges and television sets. Consumption of meat per capita was, in the 1980s, the highest in the Eastern bloc. Notwithstanding the growing debts and environmental pollution of the 1980s, this earlier, essentially difficult but nonetheless visible, relative level of achievement of the planned economy should not be completely forgotten. It was clearly not a performance comparable to that of West Germany; but it was a performance sustained under infinitely more difficult circumstances.

It should be noted, however, that the GDR had certain advantages in comparison with other East European economies. For one thing no other East European economy, with the exception of western Czechoslovakia, started its postwar experience with such a high degree of initial industrialisation and technically skilled workforce. For another, East Germany was exceptionally well-placed among Eastern bloc countries in respect of its unique relationship with West Germany. It enjoyed a special status under the 1957 Rome Treaty since the Federal Republic insisted that its trade with East Germany be considered 'domestic trade', and therefore free of tariffs and taxes. The GDR thus constituted, in effect, a secret additional member of the EC. Since around one-third of East Germany's trade with Western countries was with the Federal Republic (including West Berlin), the importance of this favourable status was not negligible. Moreover through West German links East Germany could more easily overcome bottlenecks in the supply of materials than could other Eastern bloc countries. There were other benefits from the unique German–German relationship too. West Germany sought political benefits from making favourable credit agreements with East Germany. In 1983 and 1984 large guaranteed bank loans from West Germany helped the East German economy to weather an economic storm which severely buffeted her immediate East European neighbours. West German money helped sustain the East German infrastructure, in such matters as the upkeep of autobahns to West Berlin and the restoration of historic buildings, while West German tourism (with compulsory currency exchanges) was a source of hard currency. Although difficult to quantify with any degree of exactitude, it is clear that a not inconsiderable part of East Germany's creditable economic performance had to do with its unique links with West Germany.

At the same time East Germany developed a specialised status in Comecon, developing in such areas as microelectronics and computer production, as well as retaining traditional strengths in optical and chemical concerns. But the relative success (at least in East European terms) of the East German economy was predicated on its unique position: closely related to the West, but at the same time protected from the competition of the West. After the fall of the Wall the centrally planned economy of East Germany was clearly in crisis, unable to withstand the haemorrhage of labour to the West or to compete on equal terms with technically more advanced Western products. After currency union, on a one-to-one basis, with West Germany in July 1990 the difficulties and dislocations associated with an attempted reversion to capitalist conditions became all too apparent. Attempted privatisation under the *Treuhandanstalt* fell foul of numerous complications associated with disputed property rights as well as widespread economic inefficiency and the need for modernisation. Unemployment began to rise rapidly, and associated social tensions became increasingly evident [see particularly 39].

Meanwhile in the West there were strains imposed by mass labour migration, not only from East Germany but also from elsewhere in Eastern Europe. The economy of the united Germany, with a massive imbalance between its new eastern and old western regions, clearly faced major problems. At the same time the processes of increasing integration in the European Union (formerly EEC and EC) posed further challenges and uncertainties.

(ii) Aspects of Social Structure

There were, thus, major differences between the economic structure and performance of the two economies. How far were these differences reflected in social structure and social mobility? [See generally 105, 116 and Fulbrook in 60.] Both Germanies participated in common broader trends relating to industrialisation and technological development in the later years of the twentieth century. Thus for all the very fundamental differences the social structures of the two Germanies did evince a certain comparability. Both Germanies saw a decrease in the ratio of blue-collar (manual) to white-collar (non-manual) workers. Both also saw a rise in the tertiary sector of service workers and a decline in the proportions employed in forestry and agriculture. This pattern was less marked in the East than in the West: in 1983, 16.4 per cent of West Germans were employed in the service sector and only 5.9 per cent in forestry and agriculture; while only 6.9 per cent of

East Germans were employed in the service sector and over 10 per cent remained in forestry and agriculture (compared with 17.9 per cent in 1950). The nature of the work that people actually did changed in somewhat comparable ways, although the East lagged some way behind the West in this respect.

Somewhat more marked were differences in the level of urbanisation, with an expanding population in the West increasingly living in larger urban areas while the relatively static (and sometimes declining) population of the more sparsely populated East remained to a greater extent residents of medium-sized or small communities, with less marked trends towards urbanisation. In 1950, 29 per cent of the population in both East and West Germany lived in small communities with fewer than 2000 inhabitants. In 1980, while 24 per cent of East Germans still lived in such small communities, only 6 per cent of West Germans did; by this time 74 per cent of West Germans were living in communities of over 10 000 (compared with 57 per cent of East Germans). And while East Germany's population had remained almost static, fluctuating around 17 million, West Germany's had risen by nearly 50 per cent to 61.7 million.

On the Marxist view, social classes are defined by their relationship to the means of production (ownership or non-ownership), combined with the more subjective feature of collective consciousness of common interests in opposition to antagonistic classes. In theory, then, where there is no private ownership of the means of production there ought to be no 'classes' in the pure sense, although there will still be individual differences in interest and ability. But in all state-socialist societies which have existed historically, major group-based differences in privilege, power, wealth and income persisted – although in somewhat different forms than under capitalism. And these group differences were recognised and indeed to some degree fostered by communist regimes in power. They were however (at least officially) held to be less iniquitous, more socially useful than the inequalities obtaining in capitalist societies.

In the East there was a somewhat narrower spread of income distribution than in the West, with certain crucial qualifications. An ideological commitment to greater equality was tempered, from the 1960s onwards, by a recognition of the need to attract and reward people with certain qualifications. Thus high earners included top doctors, engineers and scientists, as well as Politburo members, ministers, high-ranking officers and generals and regional industrial and political leaders. In the mid 1970s, while the average monthly income of employees in nationalised enterprises was 867 marks, top earners received salaries ranging from 2500 to as much as 10 000 marks per month. Pensioners were generally the worst off. Nevertheless, with substantial subsidies for basic foodstuffs, housing and transport, and a high proportion of two-income families in the GDR, money as such was often less important than access to Western currency or scarce goods. The long waiting lists for cars, for example, were greater stumbling blocks than any lack of money; similarly the desirable, high-quality Western goods in Intershops were available only to those who had the hard Western currency to pay for them. Moreover, as far as privileges were concerned, the privilege to travel to the West – being one of the *Reisekader* – was for most people more important than their level of income in East German marks. Political commitment, or at least conformity, was more important to acquiring privileges in the East than were income or wealth, unlike in the West.

While living standards generally were much higher in the West, there was also greater inequality of income and wealth across a broader spectrum. Although some analysts have claimed that West Germany was developing into a relatively classless society, with universal affluence allegedly obscuring social differences and regional accents denoting only area of birth, not position in a social hierarchy, nevertheless major differences in wealth and status remained. Most notably a new, ethnically distinct 'underclass' of 'guest workers' (*Gastarbeiter*) developed, predominantly employed in the most disagreeable and least well-remunerated jobs, under the worst conditions as far as such matters as employment rights, health and safety measures or level of union protection were concerned [cf. 186]. And at the top of the hierarchy the predominance of members of the old aristocracy (whether or not they had dropped the 'von' from their surnames) was still to be observed. Social mobility continued to be largely structurally induced – that is, related to changes in the class structure as a whole, with the shrinking of the agricultural and blue-collar sectors inevitably implying a degree of inter-generational mobility – with the acquisition of educational credentials to a considerable degree serving to legitimate the inheritance of social status. But with a plurality of elites – in politics, finance, business, academia, the law, the churches and other professions – there was no single route to the top in a society that might be unequal but was still relatively open. A professional and well-to-do background remained, of course, a distinct advantage – as did being male. Women in the West continued to have 'their' social class measured primarily in terms of their father's or husband's occupation. Insofar as they took up paid employment outside the home, women tended to remain in lower-status, less well-paid, often part-time or temporary employment, with minimal help by way of state nurseries or provisions for after-school childcare [77, 111].

The route to the top was rather different in East Germany [on specific groups within East German society see particularly 18 and 94]. With some exceptions, such as the pastorate and, in different ways, the medical profession, the old economic and educated bourgeoisie were transformed into the new socialist intelligentsia. The economic bourgeoisie of capitalists, large and small, of course disappeared with the nationalisation of industry and finance; and the professional classes (such as journalists, teachers, university researchers and professors, technicians and engineers) were not only reliant on the state for their professional positions, but could of course only receive the appropriate education and training through political conformity.

Under Ulbricht there were positive measures to advance previously underprivileged children from peasant and working-class backgrounds, at the expense of the middle classes (many of whom sent their children to university in the West, while the possibility was still open). State sponsorship of social mobility began to be relaxed in the 1960s, when the emphasis was put on talent in the era of scientific–technological revolution. At the same time, however, there were major structural opportunities for upward social mobility following the loss of skilled labour to the West prior to 1961. Thus the first two decades of the GDR saw what amounted to a social revolution.

This was, however, to stabilise or even stagnate in the Honecker era. By the 1970s and 1980s a certain reproduction of the class structure (inheritance of status from one generation to the next) had reappeared, with those who had been promoted at a relatively young age in the era of opportunity remaining in positions of power and frustrating the aspirations of a rising generation.

There was also a notable blockage of promotion prospects in the political hierarchy at a time when the gerontocracy showed no apparent interest in any fixed retirement age. However the most important prerequisite for social mobility was political conformity. Although Western analysts professed to see a certain tension between technical experts and party dogmatists, the system effectively prevented anyone from acquiring the appropriate educational qualifications if they were not prepared to make the necessary political commitment or evince conformity. Theology was the only possible course of study for those who wished to 'think differently'.

There has been much debate on whether there was an increasing degree of equality for women in East Germany. Certainly their participation in public life gives some grounds at least for the debate, if not the conclusions. In the Honecker era, approximately half of university students and half of the labour force were women. Particularly after the energetic introduction of pronatalist policies under Honecker (alongside the introduction in 1972 of legal abortion on demand in the first twelve weeks of pregnancy), very generous maternity benefits and extensive childcare provisions meant that it was possible, if exhausting, for women to combine the roles of mother, housewife and paid employee – and indeed it was an individual's duty to work. On the other hand, given the persistence of an unequal division of labour on the domestic front, many women experienced their role as a 'double burden', labouring under two jobs and never having time to relax. Relatively high rates of divorce and children born out of marriage reflected both the greater economic independence of East German women and the strains often experienced in marriage; but high rates of marriage and remarriage also indicated that personal relations between economically independent partners were still held in considerable esteem.

On balance it has to be said that the GDR was not a female paradise. Despite a very real ideological commitment on the part of the regime to equality of men and women in career aspirations and participation in leadership positions – rather than simply a need for maximum exploitation of labour in a demographically skewed population, with a classic postwar excess of females over males – East German women 'advanced' only a little. They remained disproportionately employed in the lower levels of all professional hierarchies, and almost completely disappeared (with individual exceptions, such as Margot Honecker) as far as the higher reaches of the political hierarchy in particular were concerned. Moreover the atmosphere of political oppression, material shortages and restricted freedom affected men and women alike, giving the lie to any notion of real 'emancipation', whether of women in particular or the 'proletariat' in general. On the other hand, however, it must also be recognised that gender was no longer the almost automatic principle of inferior status or outright exclusion from certain spheres that it had been; and although it is impossible to quantify with the precision applicable to educational qualifications or employment statistics, there does appear to have been a different flavour to gender construction in the GDR than in West Germany. A significant proportion of East German women did appear to assume that they had the right to be heard, and to speak with confidence in public as well as private.

The education systems of the two Germanies played different roles in reproducing differences in their class structures [see 75]. Education was under the control of the *Länder* in West Germany and most retained a relatively traditional selective system. The most academically gifted children attended a *Gymnasium*, a form of grammar school, at the end of which they took the *Abitur* (the rather broader equivalent of English A levels). Passing the *Abitur* gave access to university, with only a few disciplines operating a *numerus clausus* to restrict the number entering higher education. Other children attended the more vocationally oriented *Realschulen* or (to a decreasing extent) *Hauptschulen*. Emphasis on vocational training continued with efficient apprenticeship schemes and day-release courses, resulting in a well-trained workforce and the possibility of acquiring further qualifications. But for all the successes of the West German education system, it was still notable that children from working-class backgrounds appeared to have greater opportunities when the system of education was comprehensive rather than selective.

In East Germany, by contrast, after a series of reforms a system of comprehensive 'polytechnical' education, with emphasis on practical work experience as well as academic learning, was in operation for the vast majority of the population. A variety of routes into higher and further education were available even for those who did not go through the standard *Erweiterte Oberschule*

(EOS, a form of sixth-form college) for the more academically inclined. A minority of children attended a range of elite schools from an early age – either because they were identified as having, for example, particular talents in sport or music, or because they were children of the political elite. Again, whatever the educational institution, willingness at least to conform politically was the essential prerequisite of educational advancement: a university education or the chance of pursuing a chosen career was completely blocked for those who stood out as dissident or were children of, for example, prominent and outspoken Christians.

East Germany, then, was clearly not a 'classless' society in any real sense. Even the orthodox Marxists of the GDR admitted to the existence of elites and privileges [see for example 190]. They never, however, satisfactorily resolved certain problems of conceptualisation or systematic data-gathering on, for example, the loosely defined category of 'intelligentsia'. This mysteriously appeared and disappeared or was subsumed under other categories in the official statistical yearbooks; it was also used rather loosely in confidential analyses of 'moods and opinions', or popular reactions to events and topical issues.

More problematic is the task of explaining the pattern of social differentiation – particularly if the starting point is the issue of how to reduce social inequalities, or at least enhance equality of opportunity. The GDR appears to have become entrapped in a vicious circle in a number of respects. First there was the problem – in common with Western capitalist societies – of the restrictions on equality of opportunity posed by simple poverty and inequality from birth (or even conception) onwards. Innumerable studies have shown the lower birthweights, higher perinatal and infant mortality rates and lower life expectancy of children in lower social classes; these disadvantages are followed and compounded by (for whatever range of reasons) lower levels of educational attainment and correspondingly reduced chances of social mobility. In the GDR, environmental pollution seems to have exacerbated the cycle of poverty and deprivation in many areas. Secondly, the issue was overlain in state socialist societies by the extraordinary power and importance of the 'politbureaucracy'. While it is inappropriate to suggest (as some commentators did) that the GDR was characterised by a 'unitary elite', in that there was a range of politically subordinate but still privileged groups, nevertheless the ultimate power of the various branches of the party, state and security apparatus still posed an overwhelming obstacle to any attempt to achieve a society characterised by either a degree of egalitarianism or even simply equality of opportunity. The Marxist attempt to achieve a 'classless' society through the abolition of private ownership of the means of production could only hope to begin to succeed if it went hand in hand with the related notion of the 'withering away of the state' – a tendency for which state socialist societies were hardly noted.

Beyond inequalities of wealth and poverty, degrees and avenues of social mobility, living standards and life chances, there are many other aspects to society. Generation is a key and as yet inadequately explored issue in the history of the two Germanies [see for example the essays in 94 and 157; see also the intriguing interviews with members of a predominantly older generation in 146]. Both Germanies had distinctively different founding generations: the 'antifascist' credentials of the founding fathers of the GDR were in particular an important element in its legitimating myth. But both were to some degree assisted in their stabilisation by what has been called the 'Hitler Youth' generation, whose formative experiences in the Third Reich arguably predisposed them to a certain willingness to conform, to work hard and build up the new regime. The massive generational conflicts that were characteristic of West German society in the later 1960s appear to have been played out differently in the GDR [cf. the discussion of collective memory and modes of confronting the past in 61]. Despite the growth of widespread conformity if not active consensus in the 1970s and early 1980s it was the 'FDJ generation', those born into and socialised within the GDR, who were at the forefront of the demonstrations of 1989.

Regional diversity was in some respects institutionally fostered in the federal West (where it also functioned, alongside Europeanism, in place of a discredited nationalism), but it was only permitted to develop under specific conditions (as in the case of the Sorb culture) in the East. Youth subcultures developed on both sides of the Wall, but while elements among West German youth both took on transatlantic traits and at the same time critiqued aspects of Americanism, young people in the GDR were subjected to far greater official constraints. (For much of the 1950s and 1960s blue jeans and 'Rock'n'Roll' were officially seen as the outward symbols of the devil incarnate; youth continued to be a major concern of the SED.) Such comparisons and contrasts could be played out for many other topics (life cycle rituals, old age, religious subcultures, alcoholism, criminality and so on) which there is not space to explore here.

Relations between state and society were dramatically different on the two sides of the Wall. The institutionalised individualism of the capitalist West contrasted with the collectivist structures and ideology of the East. Collectivism was played out at a very early age, from the childcare practices in crèche and kindergarten through the school-based groups of Young Pioneers and Free German Youth, to the work brigades and collectives of adult working life. The vast majority of East Germans were institutionally incorporated into the social organisations of their state, in what has been called a 'politically drenched society' (*durchherrschte Gesellschaft*) [Kocka; see for example 94]. Some observers have castigated this system for its alleged mass malformation of personality [see particularly 128]. Alternatively, and from a less critical perspective, it may be pointed out that growing up in any system accustoms the majority of its people to see this as 'normal', simply 'the way things are'. Moreover the plethora of mass organisations and societies arguably anchored the East German state, with its deep roots in social life, far more effectively than the associated system of undoubted repression which has on the whole been the subject of much more general attention.

Irrespective of the bare facts of economic life and social structure, of which participants may well have been largely unaware, the nature of society in the two Germanies had diverged considerably by the time of their unification. Perceptions of culture and identity had also been transformed. It is to these more subjective issues that we now turn.

5 Patterns of Culture

Patterns of culture are notoriously difficult to define and locate. This is true to some extent of 'high culture' (literature, the performing and visual arts), and much more so of 'popular culture' in the sense of the orientations, outlooks and creative productions of subordinate social groups (including both 'mass culture' and the problematic notion of 'political culture'). Furthermore in asking about degrees of divergence between the two Germanies, can one even draw a clear baseline from which to start? There were clearly differences in religious allegiance, types of social organisation and forms of political attitude and behaviour between different social groups and in different regions of Germany before 1945. It is difficult enough to characterise the cultural patterns of any one group; to seek to do so for a whole state would seem sheer folly, if it were not for the fact that this is done all the time when people speak of, for example, 'national identity' or 'national character', or make sweeping contrasts between the supposed personality types of East and West Germans.

Nevertheless, even granted all necessary caution, there are certain diverging patterns which may be identified between the two Germanies. What makes this subject particularly interesting is the fact that on both sides the victorious powers made strenuous efforts to 're-educate' the Germans and – to a somewhat greater degree in the East than in the West – to transform the German 'personality' into a new mould. Such explicit attempts did not always produce the desired effects, while observable changes were often based on quite different factors.

(i) Official Attempts at the Transformation of the Germans

Western attempts at de-Nazification and democratisation were on the whole characterised by a degree of confusion and ultimate inefficiency. The Allies were never quite clear whether they were aiming at retribution or rehabilitation, and in the end it was the latter process which won – particularly as, in Adenauer's Germany, former 'small' Nazis (and even some less unimportant ones) were successfully reabsorbed into the mainstream of public life. In the Soviet zone the focus was less on individual personality than on structural transformation. Removing the socioeconomic base which, on the Marxist view, had given rise to Nazism was deemed more important than individual re-education. At the same time, given the associated political aim of installing communists in high places, there was also a considerable turnover of personnel, although in the East, as in the West, the importance of technical expertise necessitated the retention of many former Nazis in certain areas. In the Cold War period the two Germanies vied in attempting to discredit each other by revealing how many former Nazis held high positions in the new states [see for example 54, 61, 79, 80, 81].

In the West, apart from some rather limited early attempts to teach the Germans how to be democratic (largely on the part of the British) and how to be good managers and productivity-orientated workers (managerialist values associated with the Marshall Plan), the Allies largely left the Germans to get on with the job of becoming good democrats themselves [see for example 153]. There were constitutional restrictions on *un*democratic parties, but on the whole the limits of permissible cultural production and political activity were broad. Indeed the main constraint in the democratic capitalist West was simply material: profitability. Newspapers, for example, tended to be dominated by a few large profit-making concerns (notably, for the tabloids, the Axel Springer empire). This did not, however, preclude the publication of minority or radical views. Indeed in literature, cinema and theatre, critical views gained a certain predominance, and in the performing arts 'alternative' views were often highly subsidised. In this way a certain pluralism was even officially promoted.

In the GDR under Ulbricht, however, radical measures were adopted in the attempt to foster the development of a more uniform 'socialist personality'. The entire education system was transformed, with the abolition of private schools and the squeezing out of religious instruction already in 1946. In 1954 a secular state ceremony known as the *Jugendweihe* was introduced as a challenge and alternative to religious confirmation, further serving to differentiate between those who conformed to the atheist Marxist–Leninist world view and those who clung to their religious faith. Marxism–Leninism was a compulsory subject at all levels of the education system, from schools through further and higher education, extending even, for example, to weekend refresher courses for established members of the medical profession. Meanwhile writers and artists were also to be enlisted in the attempt to impose a new view of the world. After the Bitterfeld conference of 1959 there was to be a closer relationship between manual workers and the arts, as workers were urged to 'take up their pens' and write of their experiences, while writers were to gain experience of manual labour.

Energetic attempts to impose a new orthodoxy were relaxed somewhat in the early 1960s, but the brief moment of apparent liberalisation came to an end again in 1965. At the outset of Honecker's rule the energetic emphasis on ideological conviction appeared to decline in a context of increasingly widespread conformity. With the passage of generations, the stabilisation of the domestic and international political system and the proclaimed 'unity of economic and social policy', to a certain extent social policies based on material satisfaction in a system which was coming to be taken for granted took the place of attempts at ideological indoctrination. In the early 1970s, following Honecker's announcement of 'no taboos', there was even a certain cultural liberalisation, although this came to an end with the expulsion of the dissident guitarist and songwriter Wolf Biermann at the end of 1976. Despite the public suicide in 1976 of Pastor Brüsewitz – when he set himself on fire in protest against the regime – relations between the regime and Christians improved in the course of the 1970s, culminating in the agreement between church and state in March 1978. This accorded the church an officially tolerated status as the only independent social institution in the GDR outside the state-dominated system – a status which proved to have unintended political consequences, as we shall see in a moment.

Yet for all the changes in course and cultural policy over time, the East German regime was fundamentally based on a desire to mould people into a certain form of personality with a particular view of the world. This ideological emphasis was given visible expression in the ubiquitous banners and slogans proclaiming, for example, the undying love and friendship of East Germans for the Soviet Union, or that the regime was doing everything 'for the wellbeing of the people' (*Alles zum Wohle des Volkes*). 'The people' were of course only too well aware of propaganda and censorship. It is unlikely that the official flags and posters had much impact on people's views; and given the fact that most East Germans were able to watch Western television, they adopted quite a cynical view of their own news and current affairs programmes. The correlate of attempted indoctrination was also, of course, the systematic suppression, with greater or lesser degrees of force, of alternative, 'subversive' views. Censorship, adverse effects on career prospects, subtle pressures on family members – even the removal of dissidents' children from their families – were among the methods employed to instil fear among those who were inclined to 'think differently'. In the event, although East German culture developed in certain distinctive patterns, neither official propaganda nor suppression were entirely successful.

(ii) Literature, Culture and Religion

What were the effects of these different policies? And how far were observable, developing differences between the two Germanies the effect, not of the overt policies of the regimes, but rather of other factors, such as changing patterns of social and political experience?

As far as 'high culture' is concerned, there were clear differences which related very directly to the different political circumstances in East and West [see for example 24]. After an early, rather hesitant period in which Germans in the West had difficulty finding an authentic voice in which to speak, having to 'clear a path through the jungle' after the Nazi perversions of the language, a number of major writers began to emerge. Among those who attained international prominence for their writings, often rather critical of certain aspects of West German life, were, for example, Heinrich Böll and Günter Grass. But the West German cultural scene – in all senses – was characterised by immense diversity.

The position was very different under the more constrained political conditions obtaining in the East. Despite the repeated fluctuations in cultural policy – in which periods of relative liberalisation were followed by renewed periods of repression – and despite the assorted tactics for evading or negotiating the full effects of political censorship, or having works published in the West which were not permitted in the East, at all times East German culture was very much affected by the conditions of production. Writers may perhaps be divided into three groups: those who sustained the regime more or less wholeheartedly (perhaps with specific differences on particular issues, or private reservations about others) such as Anna Seghers or Johannes Becher; those who, while to some considerable degree being in sympathy with the overriding aims of the regime, were at least more obviously critical of certain aspects, or suffered from censorship and self-censorship at different times (Bertolt Brecht, Stefan Heym); and those for whom the constraints eventually became intolerable, and who left for the West (Jurek Becker, Monika Maron and many others). Whatever else East German literature was, it could not help but be political, even when the subject matter seemed either intensely private and personal or very far removed from the present.

Literature was for many East Germans a channel for coded discussion of present conditions, in a way which was not necessary in the West. The West had the highbrow press – newspapers such as the *Frankfurter Allgemeine Zeitung*, weeklies such as *Die Zeit* and *Der Spiegel* – in which public debates over issues of major significance could be conducted in the open and, as it were, in a 'secular' form. In the East all newspapers and magazines were either directly organs of the SED and the associated puppet parties or of the party-dominated mass organisations. A partial exception was constituted by church publications, but even these were subjected to censorship. Even the world of fiction was subjected to censorship: but there were times when certain works could be published, and also ways of saying things which allowed them to slip through.

For a long time East German writers were the focus of much, often very enthusiastic, interest in the West. But the backlash came in 1990. Christa Wolf's *Was bleibt* was a brief and at first glance seemingly innocuous work, published a decade after it was actually written, by one of East Germany's most distinguished and internationally renowned authors. But the belated publication of this autobiographical account of a day under – rather light – Stasi surveillance unleashed a controversy out of all proportion to its ostensible object. The issue revolved around whether the cultural intelligentsia in the GDR had occupied a privileged position, able to publish in and travel to the West so long as certain compromises with the regime were made, and had by this allegedly pusillanimous stance in effect helped to sustain a repressive regime in power. Those whose careers in the East had been terminated by 'going too far', such as Wolf Biermann, were bitterly critical of those who had not had the courage 'to go far enough'. In the cacophony of voices in 1990 were heard many West German critics who had never experienced, and seemed barely to understand, the kinds of constraints and pressures under which East Germans had been writing. And it should be noted that many of the critical voices in the former GDR had been seeking new ways to a better future, and were by no means simply pro-Western in their attitudes. But there was nevertheless an important underlying point. Those writers who had stayed and worked within certain limits (including a degree of self-censorship) had not in the event mounted any effective challenge to a repressive state; and the stability of the East German regime had been aided by the ease with which it could export overly critical voices to a common language community in the West, with automatic rights of citizenship, in a way that Czechoslovakia, Poland and Hungary could not. The vitriolic nature of the public debate in 1990 was indicative of a level of tension and misunderstanding of complex issues that the new Germany had to confront.

The social and political role of religion and the churches in the two Germanies diverged as a result of different political circumstances, but in comparable ways. In the West, despite the powerful institutional role and voice of the churches the salience of religion in everyday life declined for many people [see for example 174]. In the GDR, by contrast, the Protestant churches in particular came to occupy an increasingly important role in a number of – sometimes conflicting – ways (Catholics remained a rather retreatist, quiescent minority in the GDR). Subjected under Ulbricht to persecution in the 1950s, followed by a limited and rather artificial 'Christian–Marxist dialogue' in the 1960s, East German Protestants eventually came to reconsider their position. Since the 1968 constitution rendered their all-German organisation illegal (and joint meetings were in any case impracticable), East German Protestants decided in 1969 to form their own separate organisation and to adopt a more positive attitude towards working *within* (rather than 'against' or 'alongside') socialism, in Bishop Schönherr's famous formulation of 1971. Such changes in stance, and the very real importance to the East German regime of church welfare institutions (hospitals, old peoples' homes, childcare centres) and other activities, led to a change in status for the churches under Honecker, culminating in formal recognition of the church's role as an autonomous social institution in 1978.

But having gained the official status of a space in which free discussion could take place, many individual churches began to develop into centres of oppositional debate and breeding grounds of dissent. The balance began to shift in the 1980s. At first church leaders, anxious to remain on good terms with political leaders, intervened to moderate and contain dissent: religious toleration thus acted as a form of pressure valve for the regime. But from the mid 1980s onwards dissent proliferated beyond the protective (and often also constraining) bounds of the umbrella of the church. By the late 1980s there was a wide range of – not necessarily Christian – groups focusing on issues to do with human rights, peace and the environment. There were also differences within the church between 'grassroots' groups and adherents of the 'church from below', on the one hand, and on the other the more cautious or conservative members of the church hierarchy who were unwilling to put their position *vis-à-vis* the state into jeopardy. These developments were obviously the focus of much discussion among East German participants in the revolutionary autumn of 1989, when the role of Christians was very prominent (particularly in the emphasis on non-violence and the symbolism of candles).

Some commentators even termed the 1989 events a 'Protestant revolution'. However, given the very close links between members of the church leadership and the Stasi, perhaps best epitomised in the case of Manfred Stolpe, the role of religion in the GDR (both at institutional and individual levels) has been the subject of considerable controversy since the opening of the archives [see for example 16, 17, 59, 68]. Clearly the situation is one of complexity, in which no simplistic conclusions can be drawn.

(iii)   National Identity and Political Culture

What of the more ethereal or difficult to identify areas of national identity and political culture? The issue of national identity – and of overcoming the past – was high on the political agenda of both states in divided, post-Nazi Germany, and was satisfactorily resolved by neither [cf. 61, 81].

In the 1950s and 1960s the official line in the GDR was that the West was responsible for division, and that it was the East Germans who were sustaining the notion of a united German nation. Moreover, with its proud antifascist record, it was the GDR which was the historically more 'progressive' state. With international recognition of the GDR after the conclusion of *Ostpolitik* the stance changed noticeably. In the 1970s strenuous efforts were made by the East German regime to develop a sense of a separate GDR identity, based in a class theory of the nation which held that not only were there two German states, but there were now also two German nations. From the late 1970s this was accompanied by new views of German history which sought to reappropriate the whole of the German past as the GDR heritage. Figures such as Luther, Frederick the Great and Bismarck received a more sympathetic hearing than ever before in the GDR's history [see for example 20]. Visible signs of the German heritage – statues, churches, historic buildings, old town centres – began to be restored, actively preserved rather than allowed to crumble through neglect.

While East German historical writing suffered from similar pressures and constraints as literary production, and some works were the predictable product of prescribed political views, others were somewhat more interesting and – allowing for the constraints of censorship – comparable in intellectual quality to their Western counterparts [for evaluations see for example 45, 52, 61, 85, 86, 158]. After unification in 1990 there was considerable controversy, both over western decisions for mass redundancies among East German historians and over the question of who should be entitled to write GDR history [see 46, 47]. As far as the relations between professional historical writing and popular historical consciousness in the GDR is concerned, the record is complex [61]. The official founding myth of the GDR, the story of the anti-fascist heroes, was never fully swallowed; but the rehabilitation and absorption of former Nazis into East German society was relatively successful and never much of a public issue. East German citizens do not appear to have been plagued by the sort of officially cultivated culture of guilt so prevalent in the West. Most people could recognise blatant propaganda when it did not conform to everyday experience or oral traditions of popular collective memory. Politically biased histories were scarcely the sole prerogative of the East. But, under the pluralistic conditions of the West a range of different views could be published, giving rise to often heated public discussions about conflicting interpretations of the German past. In the 1950s there was a relatively conservative climate (few exiled historians chose to return to Germany) and an implicit consensus on the notion of Hitler as a 'spanner in the works', a demonic power coming out of nowhere and effectively knocking the German people off course [cf. 164, 165]. This comfortable and rather benign view of long-term trends in German history was exploded in the early 1960s, when a lively debate on Germany's role in the origins of the First World War was unleashed by the historian Fritz Fischer. In the late 1960s and 1970s historians such as Wehler began to proclaim the notion of a German *Sonderweg* or special – and distorted – path to modernity. The West German historical profession became more diverse, with a plurality of voices.

But the older conservative tones had far from died away. In the so-called 'historians' controversy' (*Historikerstreit*) during the months preceding the 1987 general election, historians such as Stürmer and Hillgruber followed Ernst Nolte's lead in seeking to construct a more 'positive' German national identity and in the process to relativise Nazi crimes [50, 106, 129]. This view was energetically contested by left–liberal intellectuals such as Jürgen Habermas and Hans-Ulrich Wehler. Heated debates also surrounded basic policy decisions, such as those concerning the foundation or slant of historical museums and exhibitions. While many West German conservatives seemed to believe that an adequate interpretation of the past or sense of national history would somehow anchor a fragile and problematic sense of contemporary national identity, other more liberal West Germans supported Habermas' notion of a more rational support of the constitution of the Federal Republic, a form of 'patriotism of the constitution'.

For all the agonising about 'overcoming the past' (*Vergangen-heitsbewältigung*) in the West and official attempts to present often distorted, black-and-white views of the past and present in the East, there is little evidence to suggest that either the debates of academics or the views promoted by governments did much to affect the sense of identity of most West and East Germans. Social and political experience, and in particular generation, seemed to be crucial factors in determining whether people saw the division of Germany as 'natural' and the two Germanies as distinct states sharing little but a common language, or as a terrible, regrettable consequence of losing the war. There was of course a fundamental asymmetry between the salience of division for West and East Germans, the former being able, quite happily, to ignore the existence of the drab and unenticing 'other Germany', while the latter were only too well aware of their effective imprisonment behind the Wall. There were also great differences with respect to generation: young West Germans in particular, with no memory of undivided Germany, tended to view the GDR as a foreign country of little personal relevance, in contrast to older citizens with more immediate memories and links. On the other hand young West Germans tended also to be among the least 'national-ist' of West Europeans, with a rather problematic relationship with the concept of national pride. Although treated very differ-ently in the two Germanies, views of the past did little to help large numbers of either East or West Germans to feel proud of their respective states: rather, in different ways on each side, it was aspects of performance in the present – particularly economic performance and material satisfaction, as well as basic freedoms of expression and travel (or lack of such freedoms) – which were fundamental.

What of patterns of political culture – and in particular the intended development of democratic and socialist personalities in East and West? As far as the West is concerned a democratic political culture shared by a majority of citizens – although not by a minority of extremists – developed in tandem with the remarkable economic recovery after the war. By the early 1960s West Germans had apparently become what political scientists called 'fair weather democrats': so long as the system produced the material goods they were prepared to support it. By the 1970s and 1980s a majority of West Germans were supporters of democracy in principle. This development – a result applauded of course by the Western Allies, who now had a reliable friend and partner in their former enemy – was a result less of the Allies' immediate postwar re-education efforts than of the simple fact that the West German political and economic systems had actually turned out to work in practice, unlike the short-lived democracy of the Weimar Republic. But the continuing regional and cultural diversity of the Federal Republic, as well as an often unremarked increase in ethnic diversity, renders problematic any overgeneralisation with respect to other aspects of popular political culture.

As far as the GDR is concerned, developments were somewhat more wayward. In the 1960s some Western analysts sought to detect growing support for the system, or at least a less grumbling willingness to make the best of an unavoidable situation; and perhaps even more East Germans experienced the closest to what might be called a 'golden age' in the GDR in the early Honecker years. International recognition, easier relations with and travel to the West, a degree of cultural liberalisation, a focus on social policies (such as housing) and consumer satisfaction, all seemed to augur well. But by the late 1970s, and certainly in the 1980s, the mood had become more depressed. It was clear that the East German economy was faltering, that environmental pollution was reaching serious proportions and that the ageing leadership would neither deal with these issues nor contemplate the kind of political liberalisation that was on the agenda elsewhere in Eastern Europe, particularly after the accession of Gorbachev to power in the USSR in 1985. So the simplistic notion of producing good socialist personalities through a combination of changed ownership of the means of production and ideological indoctrination had clearly failed. On the other hand patterns of political culture in the GDR did look distinctively different from those in the West.

As the often condescending and tendentious contrasts drawn between *Wessis* and *Ossis* in the difficult months surrounding unification indicated, it is notoriously difficult to define, let alone explain, the differences. Some aspects were quite clearly the result of particular political circumstances. It is possible that, living in a repressive regime in which there was constant pressure to conform and constant fear of Stasi observation and its possible consequences, many East Germans developed a form of dual life in a 'niche society', in the now classic formulation of Günter Gaus [63]; on the other hand, in retrospect many East Germans claim that they were able to live what they view as 'perfectly ordinary lives'. Other aspects had to do with the different socioeconomic conditions of the two Germanies described in the preceding chapter. Many East Germans were critical of what they saw as the individualistic, selfish, 'elbow society' of the capitalist West. Despite the lures of material plenty for those who were successful under capitalism, they viewed with some nostalgia the lost sense of social solidarity among subjects of the former GDR. Similarly – and to a degree at odds with this point – there were assumptions about the individual autonomy of women, who were less dependent on husbands for financial and other support than in the West. The correlate here was of course greater dependence on the state (for childcare facilities, subsidised food, guaranteed low-cost housing and so on). Expectations of the paternalistic, all-providing state were probably greater as a result.

But it would be a mistake to overgeneralise about the 'political culture of East Germans', for a variety of reasons. To start with, as in the West, cultural, class and generational differences continued to be very important. More fundamentally, East German society was, politically, deeply divided between those who actively sustained the regime, those who cooperated in some more minor way in its functioning, those who unthinkingly acquiesced and sought to live what they deemed to be quite normal daily lives, and those who in various ways made their disagreements felt – and suffered the consequences, minor or major.

Having briefly surveyed the changing patterns of politics, economy, society and culture in the two Germanies prior to 1989, it is time now to turn to the dramatic developments inaugurated by the East German revolution and the ultimate unification of what had, by 1990, become two very different Germanies.

6 The End of the Two Germanies

Less than a year after Honecker's attempted celebration of the GDR's fortieth anniversary on 7 October 1989, the GDR had ceased to exist. On 3 October 1990 the two Germanies were united in a new and enlarged Federal Republic. How can this extraordinarily rapid and dramatic transformation be explained?

There are several aspects of relevance. First, there are the long-term implications of the previous forty years of German–German relations; secondly, there are the more immediate factors involved in the East German revolution; and finally, there is the issue of how the collapse of communist rule was in the event resolved, and what shaped the processes of unification.

(i) West German Policies towards the GDR prior to 1989

German–German relations, as we have seen, were characterised by two main phases, within each of which there were minor variations [cf. 3, 8, 131].

In the first, while lip service was paid to the constitutional commitment to reunification with the East, West Germany's face was set very firmly westwards: Western integration was pursued by Adenauer at the expense of the possibility of a united Germany. Admittedly German unification at that time would have necessitated agreement to German neutrality, and – as the Cold War raged – the Western allies were not prepared either to pre-empt any decision on the military allegiance of a future, democratically elected, united German government or to run the risk of an unprotected, ill-defended Germany being overrun by the troops of what was seen as an aggressive, expansionist Soviet Union. Rather Adenauer preferred the so-called 'magnet theory'. On this view a separate West German state would ultimately be so successful and pose such an attraction that East Germans would be irresistibly drawn towards it. In the meantime the legitimacy of the GDR should not be recognised, and the West should claim to speak for all Germans in the absence of East Germans' right to voice their own opinions. Some have seen, in the final collapse of the GDR in 1989–90, a vindication of Adenauer's magnet theory.

The second major phase was inaugurated by Brandt's policy of *Ostpolitik*, characterised by 'small steps' to improve the real relationships between Germans in the two states, at the price of (implicitly) recognising the validity of the GDR's claims to be a separate state. At first this was met by strong opposition from many conservatives, who saw it as totally against German national interests and even as unconstitutional. Both politically and constitutionally, however, Brandt's policies won the day and clearly commanded considerable public support. For the following decade and a half there was broad agreement across the political spectrum that good relations should be fostered between the two German states, in the interests of improving communication at the human level (easier travel regulations. telephone links, and so on) and improving living conditions for East Germans (favourable trade and credit agreements). Some right-wing scholars, however, continued to castigate *Ostpolitik* as a means of stabilising the GDR [7]. On such a view the amelioration of domestic conditions served merely to shore up the communist regime longer than need have been the case. Others would argue, however, that the fostering of a certain consciousness of human rights and the maintenance of all-German ties were essential for the eventual successful outcome of movements for reform in the GDR.

What are the relative merits of these views on the contributions of West German policies towards the East? As far as Adenauer's policies are concerned, in a very distant sort of way his magnet theory might be said to have been proved broadly correct, in that, ultimately, political freedom and the promise of material plenty certainly proved highly attractive to a majority of Germans once they had a degree of choice in the matter. But what proved crucial was less the relative attractiveness of the West than the opening of the possibility of choice. And this had very little to do with the

Cold War fear of Soviet expansion and a lot more to do with the ending of the Cold War, inaugurated by the Soviet Union itself. This could certainly have been neither predicted nor brought about by Adenauer's policies, and thus the claims of his magnet theory must be seen as at best rather superficial. Moreover the sheer lapse of time from the 1950s to 1990 renders any putative thread of causation rather tenuous, as does the switch of policy under Brandt.

As far as Brandt's *Ostpolitik* is concerned, evaluation is more complex. On the one hand it is true that the new German–German relations did contribute to the stabilisation of the GDR under Honecker. There was not the degree of material discontent in the GDR that contributed so forcefully to the power of the Solidarity movement in Poland. Even in the more difficult circumstances of the 1980s the GDR was able to weather recession more success-fully than her Eastern European neighbours – or at least slow down the rate of economic decline – largely as a result of beneficial trade relations with West Germany (and other EC countries), consider-ably assisted by large West German loans on favourable terms. The lack of serious mass discontent thus aided the isolation of dis-senting intellectuals for a considerable time. On the other hand the public concessions that the GDR leadership had to make with respect to human rights issues – the signing of the Helsinki Final Act, the according of a degree of public tolerance to the churches, the easing of visa restrictions for travel to the West in the 1980s – all contributed to the building up of a broader basis of grassroots dissent in the 1980s. This was true with respect to organisational aspects (dissent was able to proliferate under the protection of the churches), and to the development of critiques of the regime (dis-senters could criticise realities in the light of public proclamations). Furthermore the mutual lowering of tensions and a willingness to engage in dialogue with the Soviet Union were important precon-ditions for later subsequent negotiations with the USSR. The earl-ier Western willingness to pursue possible avenues for mutual accommodation of interests, and to lower the degree of antagonism and hostility, should not be underestimated when trying to explain the new course adopted in East–West relations in the Gorbachev era.

Closer examination of the actual course of events leading to the collapse of the GDR will reveal that Western policies were prob-ably less important than developments in the Soviet Union and

Eastern Europe. Most would agree that the policies of Gorbachev were ultimately infinitely more important in bringing about the end of the division of Germany than were those of Adenauer or Brandt. As in all revolutions, however, causation is a matter of a unique combination of factors occurring at a particular historical moment. It could be argued that on balance the domestic developments in the GDR, fostered in part by Brandt's policies, were important elements in the way the East German revolution unfolded once conditions were ripe. Let us look, then, at the more immediate factors involved in the East German revolution.

(ii)   The Collapse of Communist Rule in East Germany

It was developments in Eastern Europe and the Soviet Union under the reforming leadership of Mikhail Gorbachev that proved to be vital to the collapse of the East German regime, and upon which the effectiveness of domestic movements for reform was predicated.

First, the lack of Soviet intervention – indeed the active fostering of reform movements – in other Eastern European states was a crucial factor. In particular the willingness to allow the reformist regime in Hungary to start dismantling its fortified border – the 'Iron Curtain' – with neighbouring Austria was the final precipitant of the East German revolution. Thousands of East German holidaymakers in Hungary in the summer of 1989 took the opportunity to flee westwards, while other East Germans at home, watching scenes on television of the joyful arrival of their compatriots in the freedom of the West, decided to seek refuge in West German embassies in Prague and Warsaw. It was the renewed haemorrhage of skilled labour – not seen since the erection of the Berlin Wall in 1961 – which revealed the hollowness of the SED's claim to legitimacy and initiated the ultimate collapse of communist rule in the GDR.

As far as GDR politics were concerned, there were two important sets of longer- and short-term implications of the changed climate in Eastern Europe under Gorbachev. First, Gorbachev's reforming views had for some time given general aspirations as well as specific slogans and policies to dissenters in the GDR, who nourished hopes of the introduction of restructuring and openness (*perestroika* and *glasnost*) into the neo-Stalinist style of 'actually existing socialism' under Honecker. It was these dissenters who, in the face of the escalating crisis of refugees fleeing the country, came out onto the streets demanding liberalisation and democratisation at home, so that the citizens of the GDR would want to stay and work for a better future in their own country. Against the regime's clearly spurious claims to represent the people, increasing numbers of demonstrators now proclaimed that '*We* are the People' – and 'We are staying here' [see for example 59, 163, 195].

Secondly, the changed direction of Soviet communism had, from the mid 1980s onwards, introduced new elements of discussion and incipient factionalism into the previously well-disciplined SED. Given Honecker's age and the uncertainty of the succession question, this was highly significant. In the event critiques of Honecker's inflexible responses to the mounting crises of the summer and early autumn of 1989 among Politburo members, along with Gorbachev's clear lack of support for Honecker (signalled when he visited on the occasion of the fortieth anniversary celebrations) directly led to Honecker's downfall and replacement by Egon Krenz on 18 October 1989. (Krenz in fact was something of a second choice: more in line with Gorbachev's reforming views was Hans Modrow, first secretary in Dresden but not as yet a member of the Politburo and therefore ineligible as a candidate.) Thus Gorbachev provided both the indirect stimulation and the direct impetus for a switch to a more reforming leadership in the GDR. Moreover the greater degree of debate and variegation of opinion among SED members – including regional and local leaders – played a role in the range of official responses to domestic unrest. Very important in this connection was the decision to desist from the use of force to repress unrest – the renouncing of any massacre along the lines of the Chinese suppression of the pro-democracy demonstrators in Tiananmen Square earlier in the year. The emphasis on non-violence among protesters aided the willingness to engage in dialogue on the part of certain authorities, and contributed to the – by no means inevitable – 'gentle' manner in which the revolution unfolded.

Finally, it was the USSR's – somewhat hesitant – willingness to relinquish the GDR to the West and to put an end to the Cold War which were the major preconditions for the denouement of the East German revolution in the unification of the two Germanies in 1990.

(iii)   The Unification of the Two Germanies

Unification with – or takeover by – West Germany was very far from the minds of most of those courageous individuals who spearheaded the movement for reform in the autumn of 1989. Rather, groups such as New Forum wanted to initiate discussions of shortcomings in the GDR with a view to improving conditions: they wanted free elections, freedom of the press and media, freedom to travel, freedom from the oppression of the Stasi, economic reforms, greater sensitivity to environmental matters and a reduction in militarism. Despite this list there was no agreed set of specific policies on particular issues: there was rather the desire simply that important issues should be subject to public debate and ultimately democratic decision making by a responsible and accountable government. The ideal of most was a form of (often only vaguely defined) democratic socialism.

Yet what they got, within a year, was unification with the capitalist West, on the terms of the West. How did this come about? What roles were played by different individuals – particularly the 'unification chancellor', Helmut Kohl – and by different social, economic and political factors? [See 39, 66, 67, 70, 87, 88, 92, 93, 99, 132, 149, 178.]

Kohl narrowly evaded a rather poor historical write-up. His chancellorship had been characterised by navigation around a series of scandals, such as the Flick affair, and political banana skins, such as his mismanagement of the US president's visit to SS graves at Bitburg; the popularity of Kohl's party and the prospects for re-election of a CDU–CSU–FDP coalition had been somewhat reduced by a combination of threats from the far right and the decline of the FDP alongside, for a while, the rising relative popularity of the SPD and continuing electoral support for the Greens. The West German party system had seemed to be subject to a certain new fragmentation and a degree of voter disaffection and volatility, while the chancellor had at times seemed less than agile at handling problems. Yet Kohl was saved from an unfavourable historical verdict by having the German question thrust upon him, and by seizing the opportunity with considerable astuteness and strength. His energetic intervention – and his refusal to offer unconditional economic aid at first – clearly shaped the way in which the problems consequent on the collapse of communist rule in the GDR were resolved. But these problems were not of Kohl's making; and others too played a role in the manner of their resolution. The most important factor which led to the unification of the two Germanies was economic: the GDR simply was not viable as a separate state once it was open to the competition of the capitalist West, while the latter was placed under intolerable strain by the influx of migrants from the East.

Even after the opening of the Berlin Wall on 9 November – the most symbolic concession of the would-be reformist Krenz regime, designed to symbolise the completeness of the *Wende*, or change, in domestic politics – GDR citizens continued to leave for the West, seeking better material prospects for the future. While at the end of November 1989 most observers were amazed at Kohl's 'Tenpoint Plan' for closer cooperation and eventually confederation, leading towards the political unification of the two Germanies, by February 1990 it was widely accepted that the GDR could not survive for long on its own. The continued loss of skilled labour, disruptions of production, the collapse of local administration and acute social and psychological problems amounted to a very grave crisis indeed in the GDR. The round-table government under Prime Minister Hans Modrow, which was formed after the SED renounced its constitutional claim to power in December 1989, was unable to deal with these escalating problems. But nor was the coalition government formed after the March 1990 elections – the outcome of which had been heavily influenced by the influx of West German assistance for chosen parties, and the promise of Deutschmarks arriving more speedily in the event of a victory for conservative forces sponsored by Kohl. Far from turning the East German economy around, the currency union in July 1990 only exacerbated rising unemployment and short-time working, increased bankruptcies, reduced the standards of living and heightened uncertainty about the future. Negotiations about the unification treaty were clouded too by an atmosphere of suspicion and distrust on the East German side, connected very closely with the issue of complicity with Stasi activities and the problem of what to do with the Stasi records. Under these circumstances it was scarcely surprising that experienced West German bureaucrats should make all the running, while East German politicians had little with which to bargain in the negotiations for a balanced unification treaty. Given the mounting domestic crises, even the date of unification, 3 October, was brought forward to the earliest possible moment after the resolution of external aspects of unification.

This was the other major factor involved in unification and the regaining – for the first time since the defeat of Hitler – of full sovereignty for Germany. And, as with the origins of the East German revolution, a key role was played in the resolution of the German question by the attitudes of the Soviet Union. After early prevarication on the issue of the military allegiance of a united Germany, the effective collapse in any event of the Warsaw Pact meant that the USSR had to accept united Germany's membership in a NATO which would, in the post-Cold War era, redefine its role. In the process of negotiations Germany had to make significant concessions by way of both domestic troop reductions and considerable financial and technical aid to the ailing Soviet economy, as well as paying for the removal of Soviet troops from the soil of the former GDR by 1994. These negotiations proved more complex than those with the Western powers. The three Western wartime allies – the USA, Britain and France – relatively readily gave formal approval (even if tinged by residues of anti-German sentiment and ill-founded fears of German aggression on the part of some politicians) to the unification of the two Germanies in peace and freedom. The agreements reached in the so-called '2 + 4' talks were ratified finally by the Conference on Security and Co-operation in Europe (CSCE), paving the way for formal unification ceremonies at midnight on 2–3 October 1990. Chancellor Kohl soon reaped his political reward: in the first all-German general elections, in December 1990, he was resoundingly elected chancellor of united Germany.

(iv) Unified but not United? Germany in the 1990s

As with the initial division of Germany, so the eventual unification of the two Germanies was very much a result of and essentially predicated on major changes in the international situation. The Cold War precipitated the initial division of Germany; the end of the Cold War permitted unification of what had, after four decades, become two very different Germanies. The end of division was not a simple matter of reunification but rather the creation of something very new, with its own unique characteristics and problems.

The united Germany of the 1990s was very different from the Germany which had been divided after the Second World War [see for example 112, 133, 135, 149, 172, 173, 194]. Its domestic economic and political configuration was – despite the continuity of the constitution – radically altered by unification. So too was Germany's international location. It now occupied a place in a rather different and rapidly changing European system, and faced the challenge of defining a new role within the processes of European integration which were already underway.

Almost from the moment of unification the newly sovereign Germany had to define its new political and military role in the wider international system. The Gulf War in the spring of 1991 revealed to the world that the Germans had perhaps learned their pacifist lessons too well: German aid for the United Nations forces in the military conflict against Iraq's Saddam Hussein was belated and hedged with domestic debate and ambivalence. A major political issue of 1991 became that of amending the German constitution to allow wider use of German military force. At the same time, with the effective disbanding of the Warsaw Pact and the end of the Cold War, the role of NATO itself – and Germany's place in it – would have to be redefined.

On the domestic front there were economic and social problems consequent on unification. The relatively unprotected and rapid transition from a planned to a market economy in the East, with currency union on the politically advantageous but economically disastrous one-to-one basis, soon produced rising unemployment and short-term working for an ever-growing proportion of the population. Escalating costs of reconstruction in the early 1990s led to belated but snowballing subsidies from the Bonn government, simply to keep the new provinces functioning. And for the former citizens of the GDR themselves, the strain of rising unemployment was compounded by uncertainty over such matters as subsidised housing and the continued existence of child-care facilities (leading to a drop in the birthrate of fully one half in the first two years after unification, a drop unprecedented in peacetime). This volatile combination of factors in a society undergoing rapid transformation gave rise to a range of individual psychological ills; and social tensions often also led, for some, to political extremism and racial hostility. Violent attacks on ethnic minorities increased alarmingly in the first two years after unification [cf. 120]. But such indicators of radical social distress began to wane in the mid 1990s; and for all the evident tensions between 'Easterners' and 'Westerners', the strains of unification clearly fell more heavily on some groups than others. While the generation of 40–60 year-olds were arguably the hardest hit by unemployment – too old to retrain, too young for retirement – many younger East Germans were able to benefit from the new opportunities for study, travel and free debate.

By the end of the 1990s the 'five new Länder' had received a massive if still incomplete face-lift, with resurfaced roads, renovated buildings, functioning telephone systems and new cars replacing the old polluting Trabis and Wartburgs. This face-lift was more evident in major cities and tourist destinations (particularly Berlin, designated as Germany's new capital and effectively drowned in mud and cranes in order to complete the rebuilding prior to the movement of the government, as well as removing the last traces of the Wall; but also in such places as Potsdam, Leipzig and Dresden) than it was in small towns and rural areas; and given the wave of 'Ostalgia' (*Ostalgie*, or nostalgia for the old East) that spread among East Germans who felt they were being treated as second-class citizens, the Westernisation of the ex-GDR was not universally acclaimed. Moreover, with high levels of unemployment and the simple abandonment of unviable properties, extremes of neglect and poverty were still dramatically visible alongside the new and rehabilitated. The sheer contrast between the bright new supermarkets and McDonald's fast food outlets on the one hand, and the ruins of communism on the other, rendered this still a 'foreign country' to many visitors from the West. Many West Germans still evinced little interest in or knowledge of their fellow citizens in the East.

The effective takeover of the polluted and underdeveloped Eastern provinces, with legal entanglements and property disputes delaying the process of privatisation, rendered the economy of united Germany – at least in the short term – relatively less powerful, its currency less sound, its role and aims within what became, after the Maastricht Treaty of 1992, the European Union, more problematic than that of the former West Germany alone.

The European Union was of course itself affected by the changed shape of Europe and the collapse of the Iron Curtain. Increased mobility of labour within Europe was accompanied by new controls on immigration from outside the EU. With the transition to capitalism and democracy in former Soviet bloc countries there were new debates about the 'deepening' versus the 'widening' of European integration. In this less certain context, and despite some rumblings on the fringes (including the Bavarian CSU), Germany's political leaders firmly reiterated their commitment in principle to the process of European integration. Germany played an energetic role in all aspects of this in the 1990s, including the removal of land border controls and, most notably, working towards monetary union, culminating in the introduction of the new currency, the euro, in January 1999. The effective abandonment of that symbol of West German affluence and stability, the Deutschmark, was a remarkable milestone at the close of the twentieth century. From a long-term historical point of view this pointed up notable parallels with the introduction of a customs union within the nineteenth-century German Confederation, before the first German unification of 1871. With Germany's federal tradition, as well as the taint of nationalism, Germany was well placed to understand the principles of subsidiarity and harmonisation (in a way which many British leaders could not emulate). On the other hand, as the reopened debates on entitlement to citizenship indicated, many politicians and influential opinion-shapers in Germany were still committed – as were the proverbial regulars at the beerhall *Stammtisch* – to an essentially ethnic concept of citizenship that sat uneasily alongside the millions of long-term resident 'foreign' workers and their second- and third-generation descendents in Germany.

The unification of Germany also had major implications for the character of domestic politics. Regionalism became a key issue as the successor party to the SED, the renamed PDS (Party of Democratic Socialism) became essentially a protest party representing disaffected Easterners and commanding a respectable vote in the later 1990s (around one fifth of the electorate of the eastern provinces, with higher percentages in East Berlin). At the same time the West German FDP, which had effectively held the balance of power throughout the history of West German democracy, found its support (always somewhat fragile) effectively confined to the western regions of the new Germany. Its role as coalition broker was finally shattered with the historic general election of 1998, in which, for the first time in the history of the Federal Republic, a change of government took place as a direct result of the vote of the electorate rather than the shifting allegiance of the FDP (contrast the previous changes of government in 1969 and 1982). With the chancellorship of Gerhard Schroeder, heading a 'Red–Green' coalition of SPD and Greens, a new era was clearly dawning in German politics.

In the early part of the twentieth century Germany had been characterised by domestic instability and foreign expansionism. The Second World War brought two new superpowers into Europe and dramatically altered the parameters of the 'German question'. Following the defeat of Hitler the division of Germany under the domination of the superpowers had for forty years seemed to provide some sort of solution to the 'German problem'. In the closing decade of the twentieth century the parameters began to shift again. As so often over the centuries the boundaries of 'Germany', in the essentially unstable system of states in central Europe, had been redrawn. And yet at the same time, with the effective retreat of the superpowers and the processes of closer European economic integration and political cooperation, the role of the European nation states themselves was being redefined.

7 Conclusions

One of the most interesting features of the two Germanies is that they were both founded as conscious attempts to create new – and very different – forms of society and politics on the basis of a discredited and discarded past. The division of defeated Nazi Germany, and the foundation of almost diametrically opposed capitalist and communist systems, was an experiment perhaps unparalleled in history. The record of their development is at the same time the test of that experiment: it is to a certain extent the test of social and political theory in practice.

Given the ultimate outcome – the unification of Germany on West German terms – one must obviously pose the question: what went wrong with the GDR? A state ostensibly founded on the desire to create a classless, egalitarian society in which all human beings would be emancipated from the oppressions of capitalism, and which moreover would mark a total break with the Nazi past, instead developed into a sterile dictatorship, failing even to satisfy physical, material and environmental needs, let alone the human desire for freedom and the potential for creativity and self-development.

The answer to the question of 'what went wrong?' depends partly on one's view of the Marxist ideology upon which the communist states were premised, and partly on historical analysis of the actual course of events. Some would argue that Marxism was doomed to fail in principle; others would blame the eventual collapse on a combination of, on the one hand, specific historical circumstances, and on the other the decisions and actions of those in a position to influence the course of events.

For those who hold the first view, the underpinning ideology (or would-be 'scientific' theory of society) was hopelessly wrong from the start: the experiment itself was fundamentally misguided.

On this view, for example, a centrally planned economy, with state ownership of the means of production (even if in the name of the people) could never work. Economically, without a free market to determine the balance of supply and demand there would be too many dislocations and inefficiencies to satisfy people's material needs and desires. Politically, the power of the state to determine what was deemed to be for the good of the people would condemn the latter to a permanent state of immaturity, to a 'subject' rather than 'citizen' status. Socially, the importance of power and privilege would ensure that there could never be a genuinely classless society: given the notion of an unchanging 'human nature', the idealistic goal of an equal society is unrealisable.

Others would argue that, as a set of beliefs and ideals (rather than a science), Marxism has provided a powerful vision and a set of morally informed goals. It must be the task of the historian to analyse why certain ideals were so distorted or perverted in practice; and why, ultimately, the experiment failed.

If one begins with the question of general conditions, the problems began with the earlier attempt to establish communism in a relatively backward country, namely Russia. The forced and rapid industrialisation, the concentration on heavy industry and the collectivisation of agriculture, the forcible imposition of deeply unpopular policies, the attempt to develop socialism in one country in the face of a hostile world – all these features contributed to the phenomenon of Stalinism in the USSR and the later imposition of a Stalinist regime in the Soviet zone of Germany. The hostile Cold War context and the frontline position of Germany had several consequences: fear and paranoia produced a corresponding apparatus of surveillance and repression; militarisation and expenditure on the arms race had deleterious effects on the domestic economy and consumer satisfaction; and there was a vicious circle of low support and high reliance on oppression.

Such a view focuses primarily on the supposedly inappropriate conditions in which the experiment – in itself valid – was attempted. One can also suggest that, even given the relatively restricted *Handlungsspielraum* (room for manoeuvre), the wrong decisions were taken by those in power in the GDR. Although caught between the constraints of Moscow on the one hand and the limits of exploitability of the labour force on the other, the SED leadership might on occasion have made other decisions with less deleterious consequences. Thus, for example, had the New Economic System been allowed time to develop (rather than being both distorted in practice and truncated in timescale), a stronger and more flexible economy might have emerged, better able to cope with the challenges of the late 1970s and 1980s. Similarly had Honecker not insisted on the economically non-viable combination of massive consumer subsidies and continued investment in superannuated heavy industry as well as microelectronics, wilfully ignoring all warning signs and refusing even to admit the need for, let alone seriously consider, possible plans for reform, the economy might not have collapsed so rapidly in the 1980s.

It is, however, hard to see how, unless the GDR was both as economically successful and as politically open as its Western twin, it could at any time have faced an open western border while the West still offered automatic citizenship rights. It would have taken an exceedingly prosperous as well as egalitarian and democratic communism to survive the fall of the Wall.

Given what did actually happen, some would wish to insert into the debate the question of the positive 'achievements' of the GDR, or 'what remains' (to adopt the increasingly popular title of Christa Wolf's contentious novella). One obvious candidate for discussion – particularly given the very heated debates on abortion – was the role of women. Even if the greater relative equality of women with men in the GDR is dismissed as greater equality of misery rather than anything approaching emancipation, the social policies which enhanced women's freedom of choice (particularly the generous childcare provision) and raised their educational and career aspirations, as well as their sense of self-confidence and self-respect, are pointed to as factors not to be ignored in the final balance sheet. So too are the subsidised rents and food prices, the guaranteed housing and employment, the provision of adequate pensions and a universally available health service – even if, again, these are qualified in terms of rather minimal standards or a low quality of life. More ethereally, some have praised a certain social solidarity among people subjected to common constraints and pressures, in contrast to the materialist, individualist 'elbow society' of the capitalist West, and have valued the qualities of GDR cultural, moral and religious life. But these are diffuse and not easily quantifiable facets which are generally inserted into a balance sheet which overwhelmingly emphasises the immoral and repressive aspects of the regime.

We shall return to the wider implications of these debates in a moment. But it is important now to consider the case of West Germany. Why was it that democracy in the Federal Republic was, in contrast to its Weimar predecessor, so stable? A number of factors appear to be important.

The settlement after the Second World War, as far as the Western zones were concerned, contrasted markedly with the treatment meted out in the Versailles Treaty of 1919. Although the post-1945 settlement was in some respects harsher (occupation, division, loss of sovereignty), the early commitment of the Western Allies to economic reconstruction on firm foundations constituted a major, indeed fundamental difference. And it was on the early spectacular success of the West German economy, as well as its commitment to Western integration on the lines of the American conception of the postwar world order, that the stability of West German democracy in the early years was based. As far as domestic factors were concerned, constitutional provisions (the outlawing of anti-democratic parties, the 5 per cent hurdle) were of some importance. But probably more important was the way in which the structures of West German political and economic life gained the support and commitment of key elite groups. It was not only politicians who came to support the new system in principle: it was also the leaders of business and industry, as well as the trade unions, which – for all the differences over degrees of codetermination or social partnership – found that the corporatist structures actually worked and helped to protect their interests, at least within a rapidly growing economy. With the passage of time, as West Germany became a respected partner in the Western alliances and as a generation came to maturity who took democratic politics for granted, the system was sufficiently well-anchored to weather greater economic difficulties. It was also sufficiently secure to cope with challenges from political extremists at the margins, and to conduct with a modicum of tolerance and at times acerbic public debate over its relations with its past.

As far as the outcome in 1989–90 is concerned, however, at least two notes of caution must be struck with respect to the apparent 'winner' of the historical contest. For one thing, at the close of the 1980s it was less that capitalism 'won' than that communism collapsed, for a range of factors more related to events in the Soviet bloc than the West. For another, with respect to criticisms of Marx's ideas, neither East German 'communism' nor West German 'capitalism' were in actuality anything like the pure types described by Karl Marx. Bureaucratic state socialism in innumerable respects perverted the ideals embodied in Marx's vision of communism. Meanwhile the capitalism of the late twentieth century was so modified, with so many safeguards and welfare provisions and so much state intervention, that the worst effects of a capitalist free market were mitigated. History had simply moved on from the period in which Marx worked out his ideas – and history did not thus constitute any real test of Marx's global theories (which were in any event riddled with ambiguities which cannot be explored here).

Moreover, despite the appearance of having 'won' the historical contest (not least in the terms of unification in 1990), and despite its very real achievements in terms of economic productivity and democratic stability, West Germany has also been evaluated in the light of differing criteria. Crass materialism has consistently been criticised from the 1950s onwards; the reincorporation of former Nazis and the difficulty of coming to terms with the Nazi past have been the subject of much controversy; the reproduction of social inequalities, the hostile treatment of ethnic minorities or 'foreign' workers and the relative poverty and neglect of many pensioners have aroused criticism. But a fundamental difference is that such criticisms can be raised – and fought out – within the terms and parameters of the democratic political system itself. Pressure groups and parties can seek to change the conditions they criticise. Furthermore West German democracy has enjoyed the considerable good fortune of being based in a powerful and well-run economy, where economic growth and increased prosperity for all have served to disguise the persistence of relative social inequalities. Despite all the very real problems of a social market form of capitalism – the business cycle, the existence of unemployment, inequality of life chances, the persistence of poverty alongside extraordinary wealth – for many the prospect of personal advancement and a high standard of living has outweighed the risks associated with such a system. And arguments about contentious issues – confronting or commemorating the Nazi past, renegotiating citizenship entitlement, environmental pollution and many more – can be debated in a public sphere in which many voices can be raised and heard. Critique is the concomitant of action for change.

It is clear that any historical analysis of the two Germanies will easily be tempted into the shoals of moral and political evaluation. But the task of the historian is essentially to analyse and explain, not to evaluate. Stepping outside the self-understandings of political actors in the drama of the two Germanies, can we develop any general conclusions on the basis of the analysis presented in the preceding chapters?

First, no society can be viewed purely in self-contained terms. Both Germanies can only be understood as part of a wider international system – political, military and economic. Their relative successes and failures in different spheres have much to do with the wider systems of which they were a part and in which they played distinctive roles. The GDR's longevity and ultimate end had, very obviously, much to do with the interests and capacities of the Soviet Union. Its modest economic success (in comparison with its East European neighbours) also had not a little to do with its special relationship with the Federal Republic. But equally the stability of West German democracy had much to do with its economic success, predicated initially on American rebuilding after the war and premised further on a developing role in both world markets and the European Community. Neither Germany can be explained purely in terms of its own particular political and economic system, without reference to the wider conditions of Europe and the world. So neither system, in the abstract, can be adjudicated solely on its record in its particular part of divided Germany.

Secondly, and partly related to this, the kind of global comparison of systems that used to be popular should be abandoned in favour of a more differentiated approach to analysis of specific aspects and areas. Catch-all concepts such as 'capitalism', 'communism' and 'totalitarianism' will not serve to unlock the secrets of detailed historical developments. 'Capitalism' was *not* associated with successful democracy in the Weimar Republic or the Third Reich; its political supporters still have to explain why market economies are not always connected with political freedom. Nor is the picture any easier with respect to the allegedly intrinsic economic shortcomings of communism, or the repression associated with notions of 'totalitarianism'. For example there is little point in appealing to material discontent as a key causal factor in explaining the origins of the East German revolution, since it had been insufficient to upset the political system over the previous forty years. Similarly the use of force as a means of controlling the population varied over time – and, ironically, the repressive capacity of the GDR was at its greatest at precisely the time of its collapse. To appeal to 'repression' as an unchanging factor is to miss many nuances and variations. Rather, unique combinations of factors under changing circumstances must be considered to explain particular eventuations.

Certain elements of such a multifaceted approach to the two Germanies have been suggested above. With respect to West Germany, distinctive features of its social market economy and constitution, under favourable international circumstances, aided the development of a relatively stable democracy characterised by widespread, if not universal, material affluence and a degree of critical debate. For all its acknowledged shortcomings the West German system – for a variety of reasons – appeared to work. With respect to East Germany, a peculiar combination of changing domestic factors produced a certain stability over forty years – a record not to be forgotten in the light of the GDR's ultimate collapse. In the 1950s a combination of repression and the exclusion of domestic dissent laid the foundations for the 'established phase' which followed the construction of the Wall and the achievement of international recognition after *Ostpolitik*. During the 1960s and 1970s intellectual dissent was relatively easily isolated or exiled, and modest rates of economic growth produced at least quiescence on the part of the majority of the population, at a time when there appeared to be few viable alternatives. The regime's experiment with a greater latitude of toleration *vis-à-vis* the church from the late 1970s even gave some cause to hope for a degree of liberalisation in time. Increasing pressure for change from within was fuelled by the accession of Mikhail Gorbachev to power in the Soviet Union, with the introduction of major reforms there and elsewhere in Eastern Europe – which were, however, resisted by Honecker and the old guard leadership. East German hopes for reform were dashed when the rapid proliferation of domestic dissent gave rise to increased use of force and suppression on the part of a rattled regime in the later 1980s. The opening of the Iron Curtain between Austria and Hungary in the summer of

95

1989 came at a time of peculiar domestic lability in the GDR. The decisive factors affecting the ultimate outcome were, on the one hand, for the first time since 1961, the possibility of flight to the West, combined with, on the other, the refusal on the part of the Soviet Union to countenance or support the use of force in the suppression of more activist movements for reform within the GDR. The result, once the Wall fell, was to be the end of the GDR.

It has not been possible in this brief compass to do more than touch on the many aspects and approaches relevant to interpreting the two Germanies. This is moreover a very recent past, analysis of which has political implications in the present. Since unification the availability of new material has led to new perspectives and new debates on the tangled, contentious histories of the two Germanies. The extraordinary, unparalleled experiment of founding two such very different states and societies, a capitalist democracy and a communist state, on the soil of defeated Nazi Germany, and then of engaging in the unprecedented process of subsequently recombining them, is certain to remain a subject of both lively academic controversy and political engagement.

Select Bibliography

This bibliography has been substantially pruned since the first edition of this work in order to take account of at least some of the more recent literature without growing totally out of proportion. Certain older works have been retained, either because they remain important or because they are referred to in the text as illustrative of a particular approach or issue. Some English and German works have been annotated, to assist in selection for particular purposes.

Those English-language texts which might form particularly useful components of a short bibliography for teaching purposes have been marked with an asterisk; these generally also contain suggestions for further reading. The bibliography remains highly selective, even with respect to more recent works, where frequently only one or two significant or typical works have been listed for a topic where a great deal more has been published. In particular there has been an explosion of literature on the GDR since unification. Much of the most interesting recent research is in German, only a small selection of which could be included; again the references in these will guide the reader further. This is thus intended as a purely introductory, rather than comprehensive, bibliography.

*[1]   R. Alter and P. Monteath (eds), *Rewriting the German Past* (New York: Humanities Press, 1997). Useful collection of post-*Wende* essays on a range of facets of recent German history, introducing key debates and further reading.

[2]   R. Andert and W. Herzberg, *Der Sturz: Erich Honecker im Kreuzverhör* (Berlin and Weimar: Aufbau Verlag, 1990). Honecker's own view of his downfall, elicited in interview by two journalists.

[3]   T. Garton Ash, *In Europe's Name* (New York: Random House, 1993).

[4]   T. Garton Ash, *The File* (London: HarperCollins, 1997). Personal account of encounters with some of those who spied on Garton Ash (to little effect) for the Stasi.

*[5]   M. Balfour, *Germany: The Tides of Power* (London: updated edn, Routledge, 1992). Useful, chronologically organised narrative, updated.

*[6]   A. Baring, *Uprising in East Germany* (New York: Cornell University Press, 1972). Remains a classic account, despite more recent variations on the themes.

[7]   D. Bark and D. Gress, *A History of West Germany*, 2 vols (Oxford: Basil Blackwell, 1989). A rather disjointed and highly politicised Cold War blockbuster.

[8]   A. Bauerkämper, M. Sabrow and B. Stöver (eds), *Doppelte Zeitgeschichte* (Berlin: Dietz Verlag, 1998). A useful collection of essays providing new perspectives on the divided history of united Germany.

[9]   A. Bauerkämper, J. Danyel, P. Hübner and S. Roß (eds), *Gesellschaft ohne Eliten?* (Berlin: Metropol, 1997).

[10]   T. Baylis, *The Technical Intelligentsia and the East German Elite* (Berkeley: University of California Press, 1974). Convincing early reply to Ludz's influential conception of the 'counter-elite'.

[11]   M. Beleites, *Untergrund. Ein Konflikt mit der Stasi in der Uran-Provinz* (Berlin: BasisDruck, 1992). Personal account by a former East German environmental activist.

[12]   W. Benz (ed.), *Die Bundesrepublik Deutschland*, 3 vols (Frankfurt: Fischer, 1983).

[13]   S. Berger, *The Search for Normality* (Oxford: Berghahn, 1997). Lively, detailed and opinionated survey of recent German historiographical trends.

[14]   V. Berghahn, *The Americanisation of West German Industry 1945–73* (Leamington Spa: Berg, 1986).

*[15]   V. Berghahn, *Modern Germany* (Cambridge: Cambridge University Press, 2nd edn, 1987). An excellent textbook, weighted towards the earlier part of the century and West German history.

[16]   G. Besier, *Der SED-Staat und die Kirche* (Munich: C. Bertelsmann Verlag, 1993). Detailed indictment of compromises made by the East German churches with the communist state.

[17]   G. Besier and S. Wolf (eds), *'Pfarrer, Christen und Katholiken'. Das Ministerium für Staatssicherheit der ehemaligen DDR und die Kirchen* (Neukirchen: Neukirchener Verlag, 2nd edn, 1992). Revealing collection of documents about the Stasi infiltration of East German churches.

[18]   R. Bessel and R. Jessen (eds), *Die Grenzen der Diktatur* (Göttingen: Vandenhoeck and Ruprecht, 1996). Essays on the 'limits of the dictatorship' and the social history of the GDR.

[19]   K. von Beyme and H. Zimmermann (eds), *Policymaking in the German Democratic Republic* (Aldershot: Gower, 1984).

[20] J. H. Brinks, *Die DDR-Geschichtswissenschaft auf dem Weg zur deutschen Einheit* (Frankfurt: Campus, 1992).

[21] S. Bulmer and W. Paterson, *The Federal Republic of Germany and the European Community* (London: Allen & Unwin, 1987).

[22] Bürgerkomitee Leipzig (ed.), *Stasi Intern. Macht und Banalität* (Leipzig: Forum Verlag, 1991).

[23] R. Burns and W. van der Will, *Protest and Democracy in West Germany: Extra-Parliamentary Opposition and the Democratic Agenda* (London: Macmillan, 1988).

*[24] R. Burns (ed.), *German Cultural Studies* (Oxford: Oxford University Press, 1995). Useful overview from an interdisciplinary perspective.

[25] E. Carter, *How German is She? Postwar West German Reconstruction and the Consuming Woman* (Ann Arbor: University of Michigan Press, 1997).

[26] D. Cesarani and M. Fulbrook (eds), *Citizenship, Nationality and Migration in Europe* (London: Routledge, 1996).

[27] D. Childs, *The GDR: Moscow's German Ally* (London: George Allen & Unwin, 1983). Now somewhat dated, but a classic English textbook on the GDR in its time.

[28] D. Childs (ed.), *Honecker's Germany* (London: Allen & Unwin, 1985).

[29] D. Childs, T. Baylis and M. Rueschemeyer (eds), *East Germany in Comparative Perspective* (London: Routledge, 1989).

[30] D. Childs and J. Johnson, *West Germany: Politics and Society* (London: Croom Helm, 1981).

[31] D. Childs and R. Popplewell, *The Stasi. The East German Intelligence and Security Service* (Basingstoke: Macmillan, 1996). Very basic English-language introduction to this important topic (upon which there is much more in German).

[32] S. Cobler, *Law, Order and Politics in West Germany* (Harmondsworth: Penguin, 1978). Revealing not only about its ostensible topic, but also about the West German *Zeitgeist* at the time of writing.

*[33] D. P. Conradt, *The German Polity* (London: Longman, 4th edn, 1989. Excellent introduction to West German politics.

[34] R. Dahrendorf, *Society and Democracy in Germany* (London: Weidenfeld and Nicolson, 1968). Early and important statement about the alleged 'modernising' contribution of the Third Reich, viewing West German history in longer-term perspective.

[35] *DDR-Handbuch* (Köln: Verlag Wissenschaft und Politik; various editions). Indispensable handbook.

[36] *DDR – Wer war wer. Ein biographisches Lexikon* (Berlin: Ch. Links Verlag, 1992). One of several useful biographical reference works.

[37] A. Deighton, *The Impossible Peace* (Oxford: Clarendon Press, 1990).

[38]   M. Dennis, *German Democratic Republic* (London: Pinter, 1988).
*[39]   M. Dennis, *Social and Economic Modernisation from Honecker to Kohl* (London: Pinter, 1993). Informative survey of much more than the title implies.
[40]   Deutscher Bundestag (ed.), *Materialien der Enquete-Kommission 'Aufarbeitung von Geschichte und Folgen der SED-Diktatur in Deutschland'*, 9 vols (Frankfurt-am-Main, 1995). 'Expert' reports and contentious debates on aspects of East German history produced for the Federal German parliament.
[41]   Deutsches Institut für Wirtschaftsforschung Berlin (ed.), *Handbuch DDR-Wirtschaft* (Hamburg: Rowohlt, 4th edn, 1984).
[42]   *Deutschland-Archiv* (Cologne: Verlag Wissenschaft und Politik). A key periodical on GDR history.
[43]   T. Diedrich, *Der 17. Juni 1953. Bewaffnete Gewalt gegen das Volk* (Berlin: Dietz Verlag, 1991).
[44]   C. V. Ditfurth, *Blockflöten. Wie die CDU ihre realsozialistische Vergangenheit verdrängte* (Cologne: Kiepenhauer and Witsch, 1991).
[45]   A. Dorpalen, *German History in Marxist Perspective: The East German Approach* (London: I. B. Tauris, 1985).
[46]   R. Eckert, W. Küttler, and G. Seeber (eds), *Krise – Umbruch – Neubeginn. Eine kritische und selbstkritische Dokumentation der DDR-Geschichtswissenschaft 1989/90* (Stuttgart: Klett-Cotta, 1992)
[47]   R. Eckert, I.-S. Kowalczuk and I. Stark (eds), *Hure oder Muse? Klio in der DDR* (Berlin: Berliner Debatte, 1994).
*[48]   L. Edinger, *West German Politics* (New York: Columbia University Press, 1986). Useful introduction by an American political scientist.
[49]   G. E. Edwards, *GDR Society and Social Institutions* (London: Macmillan, 1985). Extraordinarily rosy view by a sympathiser.
[50]   Richard J. Evans, *In Hitler's Shadow* (London: I. B. Tauris, 1989). Rapid guide to the *Historikerstreit*.
[51]   C. Fink, P. Gassert and D. Junker (eds), *1968: The World Transformed* (Cambridge: Cambridge University Press, 1998).
[52]   A. Fischer and G. Heydemann (eds), *Geschichtswissenschaft in der DDR* (Berlin: Duncker and Humblot, 1988).
[53]   T. Forster, *The East German Army* (London: George Allen & Unwin, 5th edn, 1980).
[54]   N. Frei, *Vergangenheitspolitik* (Munich: C. H. Beck, 1996). Illuminating analysis of ways of dealing with the past in Adenauer's Germany.
[55]   K. W. Fricke, *Opposition und Widerstand in der DDR* (Cologne: Verlag Wissenschaft und Politik, 1984).
[56]   K. W. Fricke, *MfS Intern* (Cologne: Verlag Wissenschaft und Politik, 1991). The books by Fricke [55 and 56] remain classics; the latter has been usefully updated.
[57]   R. Fritsch-Bournazel, *Confronting the German Question* (Oxford: Berg, 1988); see also *Europe and German Unification* (Oxford: Berg, 1992).

[58]   M. Fulbrook, *Germany 1918–1990: The Divided Nation* (London: Fontana, 1991).
*[59] M. Fulbrook, *Anatomy of a Dictatorship: Inside the GDR, 1949–1989* (Oxford: Oxford University Press, 1995). Analysis of changing patterns of political culture in the GDR; particular emphasis on church–state relations and the emergence of 'political activism' in the 1980s.
*[60] M. Fulbrook (ed.), *German History since 1800* (London: Arnold, 1997), Part IV.
[61]   M. Fulbrook, *German National Identity after the Holocaust* (Cambridge: Polity, 1999). Comparison of the ways in which a common past was differently presented and new identities constructed in the two German states.
[62]   J. Gauck, *Die Stasi-Akten. Das unheimliche Erbe der DDR* (Hamburg: Rowohlt, 1991). Interesting guide by the former East German pastor charged with the duty of overseeing the Stasi archival legacy.
[63]   G. Gaus, *Wo Deutschland liegt* (Munich: dtv, 1986). Classic statement of 'niche society' thesis by a former West German 'representative' (equivalent to an ambassador in a foreign country) in the GDR.
[64]   *GDR Monitor, German History, German Politics, German Studies Review*. Useful English-language periodicals with detailed articles on both Western and Eastern Germany and occasional special issues.
[65]   D. Gill and U. Schroeter, *Das Ministerium für Staatssicherheit. Anatomie des Mielke-Imperiums* (Berlin: Rowohlt, 1991).
*[66] G.-J. Glaeßner, *The Unification Process in Germany: From Dictatorship to Democracy* (London: Pinter, 1992).
*[67] G.-J. Glaeßner and I. Wallace (eds), *The German Revolution of 1989* (Oxford: Berg, 1992). Useful collection of essays.
*[68] R. Goeckel, *The Lutheran Church and the East German State* (Ithaca, NY: Cornell University Press, 1990). Researched prior to the fall of the Wall, but remains a good English-language analysis of the main parameters of church–state relations in the GDR.
[69]   H. Gotschlich (ed.), *'Links und links und Schritt gehalten . . .' Die FDJ: Konzepte – Abläufe – Grenzen* (Berlin: Metropol Verlag, 1994).
*[70] K. Gransow and K. Jarausch, *Uniting Germany: Documents and Debates* (Providence, RI, and Oxford: Berghahn, 1994).
[71]   P. Grieder, *The East German Leadership, 1946–73: Conflict and Crisis* (Manchester: Manchester University Press, 1999).
[72]   J. Hacker, *Deutsche Irrtümer: Schönfärber und Helfershelfer der SED-Diktatur im Westen* (Frankfurt-am-Main and Berlin: Ullstein, 1992). Argues against western woolly-headed liberal academics who were allegedly taken in by SED propaganda during the period of détente.

[73] M. Hagen, *DDR – Juni '53* (Stuttgart: Steiner, 1992). Eyewitness memories and other material on the June uprising.
[74] K. Hager, *Erinnerungen* (Leipzig: Faber and Faber, 1996).
[75] A. Hearndon (ed.), *Education in the Two Germanies* (Oxford: Basil Blackwell, 1974).
[76] H. Heitzer, *GDR: An Historical Outline* (Dresden: Verlag Zeit im Bild, 1981). Official SED history of the GDR, in English.
[77] G. Helwig, *Frau und Familie* (Köln: Verlag Wissenschaft und Politik, 2nd edn, 1987).
[78] Rüdiger Henkel, *Im Dienste der Staatspartei. Über Parteien und Organisationen der DDR* (Baden-Baden: Nomos Verlag, 1994). One of an increasing number of basic informative (but non-analytical) guides to organisations and groups in the GDR.
[79] U. Herbert, *Best* (Bonn: Dietz Verlag, 1996).
[80] U. Herbert and O. Groehler, *Zweierlei Bewältigung: Vier Beiträge über den Umgang mit der NS-Vergangenheit in beiden deutschen Staaten* (Hamburg: Ergebnisse Verlag, 1992).
[81] J. Herf, *Divided Memory* (Cambridge, Mass.: Harvard University Press, 1997).
[82] M. Hogan, *The Marshall Plan* (Cambridge: Cambridge University Press, 1987).
[83] P. Hübner, *Konsens, Konflikt, und Kompromiß* (Berlin: Akademie Verlag, 1995).
[84] W. Hülsberg, *The German Greens: A Social and Political Profile* (London: Verso, 1988).
[85] G. Iggers, K. Jarausch, M. Middell and M. Sabrow (eds), *Die DDR-Geschichtswissenschaft als Forschungsproblem* (Munich: Oldenbourg, 1998; *Historische Zeitschrift*, Beiheft 27).
*[86] G. Iggers, *Marxist Historiography in Transformation* (Oxford: Berg, 1991).
*[87] H. James and M. Stone, *When the Wall came down* (London: Routledge, 1992). Selection of contemporary political and scholarly reactions.
*[88] K. Jarausch, *The Rush to German Unity* (Oxford: Oxford University Press, 1994). Clear account of events.
[89] K. Jarausch (ed.), *Zwischen Parteilichkeit und Professionalität. Bilanz der Geschichtswissenschaft der DDR* (Berlin: Akademie Verlag, 1991).
[90] I. Jeffries and M. Melzer, *The East German Economy* (London: Croom Helm, 1987).
[91] E. Jesse (ed.), *Bundesrepublik Deutschland und Deutsche Demokratische Republik: Die beiden deutschen Staaten im Vergleich* (Berlin: Colloquium Verlag, 3rd edn, 1982).
[92] E. Jesse and A. Mitter, *Die Gestaltung der deutschen Einheit* (Bonn: Bundeszentrale für politische Bildung, 1992).
[93] C. Joppke, *East German Dissidents and the Revolution of 1989* (Basingstoke: Macmillan, 1995).

[94]   H. Kaelble, J. Kocka and H. Zwahr, *Die Sozialgeschichte der DDR* (Stuttgart: Klett-Cotta, 1994). Excellent collection of essays on a range of aspects of GDR social history, including both specific social groups or themes and more general interpretations.

[95]   Monika Kaiser, *Machtwechsel von Ulbricht zu Honecker. Funktionsmechanismen der SED-Diktatur in Konfliktsituationen 1962 bis 1972* (Berlin: Akademie Verlag, 1997).

[96]   P. Katzenstein, *Policy and Politics in West Germany: The Growth of a Semi-sovereign State* (Philadelphia: Temple University Press, 1987).

[97]   P. Katzenstein (ed.), *Industry and Politics in West Germany* (Ithaca: Cornell University Press, 1989).

[98]   L. Kettenacker, *Germany since 1945* (Oxford: Oxford University Press, 1997).

[99]   D. Keithly, *The Collapse of East German Communism. The Year the Wall Came Down* (Westport, CT: Praeger, 1992).

[100]   D. Keller, H. Modrow and H. Wolf (eds), *Ansichten zur Geschichte der DDR* (Bonn, Berlin: PDS/Linke Liste im Deutschen Bundestag, 1993). Reply to the Federal German parliament's inquiry from a PDS (Communist successor party) perspective.

[101]   O. Kirchheimer, 'Germany: the vanishing opposition', in R. A. Dahl (ed.), *Political Oppositions in Western Democracies* (New Haven, CT: Yale University Press, 1966). Classic political science essay making the case for convergence of main parties in West German democracy.

[102]   *Kleines Politisches Wörterbuch* (Berlin: Dietz-Verlag, 3rd edn, 1978). Useful statement of official GDR views on many matters.

[103]   C. Kleßmann, *Die doppelte Staatsgründung* (Göttingen: Vandenhoeck and Ruprecht, 1982).

[104]   C. Kleßmann, *Zwei Staaten, eine Nation: Deutsche Geschichte 1955–70* (Göttingen: Vandenhoeck and Ruprecht, 1988; 2nd edn, Bonn, 1997). This and the previous collection [103] are indispensable sets of primary sources in German with consistently illuminating commentaries by Kleßmann.

[105]   K. Kleßmann and G. Wagner (eds), *Das gespaltene Land* (Munich: C. H. Beck, 1993). An attempt at adding a social history dimension to the previous two collections.

*[106] J. Knowlton and T. Cates, *Forever in the Shadow of Hitler?* (New Jersey: Humanities Press, 1993). English translation of Piper collection of *Historikerstreit* documents.

[107]   J. Kocka (ed.), *Die DDR als Geschichte* (Berlin: Akademie Verlag, 1994).

[108]   J. Kocka, *Historische DDR-Forschung* (Berlin: Akademie Verlag, 1993). This and the previous collection present early fruits of promising research at what became the (at first

controversial, but highly productive) *Zentrum für Zeithistorische Studien* in Potsdam.

[109] P. Ködderitsch and L. Müller, *Rechtsextremismus in der DDR* (Göttingen: Lamuv Verlag, 1990).

[110] E. Kolinsky (ed.), *The Greens in West Germany* (Oxford: Berg, 1989).

[111] E. Kolinsky, *Women in West Germany* (Oxford: Berg, 1989).

[112] E. Kolinsky (ed.), *Between Hope and Fear: Everyday life in Postunification East Germany. A Case Study of Leipzig* (Keele: Keele University Press, 1995).

*[113] J. Kopstein, *The Politics of Economic Decline* (Chapel Hill: University of North Carolina Press, 1997). Excellent analysis of the interplay between SED economic strategies and constraints from 'above' (Moscow) and 'below' (the working classes).

[114] I.-S. Kowalczuk, A. Mitter and S. Wolle (eds), *Der Tag X. 17. Juni 1953* (Berlin: Ch. Links Verlag, 1995).

[115] A. Kramer, *The West German Economy* (Oxford: Berg, 1991).

[116] J. Krejci, *Social Structure in Divided Germany* (London: Croom Helm, 1976). Now somewhat dated, but an early and still interesting attempt at comparing the social structures of the two Germanies.

[117] E. Krenz, *Wenn Mauern fallen* (Vienna: Neff, 1990).

[118] F. Kroh (ed.), *'Freiheit ist immer Freiheit . . .' Die Andersdenkenden in der DDR* (Berlin: Ullstein, 1988).

[119] M. Krüger-Potratz, *'Anderssein gab es nicht'* (Münster: Waxmann, 1991).

[120] H. Kurthen, W. Bergmann and R. Erb (eds), *Antisemitism and Xenophobia in Germany after Unification* (Oxford: Oxford•University Press, 1997). Essays exploring aspects of anti-Semitism in Germany, including historical perspectives since 1945.

[121] W. Leonhard, *Child of the Revolution* (London: Collins, 1957). Classic eyewitness account of the communist takeover of Eastern Germany after the war.

[122] G. Lepton and M. Melzer, *Economic Reform in East German Industry* (London: Oxford University Press, 1978). Account of the New Economic System.

[123] W. Loth, *Stalin's Unwanted Child: The Soviet Union, the German Question, and the founding of the GDR* (Basingstoke: Macmillan, 1998; orig. German 1996). Controversial reinterpretation of the origins of the GDR.

[124] P. C. Ludz, *The Changing Party Elite in East Germany* (Cambridge, Mass.: MIT Press, 1972). Classic statement of an alleged switch in the GDR from a 'totalitarian' regime to one characterised by 'consultative authoritarianism', and the supposed emergence of a technocratic 'counterelite'.

[125] P. C. Ludz, 'East Germany: Continuity and change since Ulbricht', *Problems of Communism*, vol. 21 (1972), pp. 56–67.

[126]   P. C. Ludz, *The GDR from the Sixties to the Seventies* (Harvard Center for International Affairs: Occasional Papers in International Affairs, no. 26, Nov. 1970).

[127]   K. Maase, *BRAVO Amerika. Erkundungen zur Jugendkultur der Bundesrepublik in den fünfziger Jahren* (Hamburg: Junius Verlag, 1992).

*[128]   H.-J. Maaz, *Behind the Wall* (London: W. W. Norton, 1995). Translation of Maaz's notorious 'psychogramme' of East Germans (including the alleged psychological and political consequences in adulthood of collectivised potty training).

*[129]   C. Maier, *The Unmasterable Past: History, Holocaust, and German National Identity* (Cambridge, Mass.: Harvard University Press, 1988). The *Historikerstreit* and much else of interest about (West) German historical consciousness; a broader scope than Evans [50].

*[130]   C. Maier, *Dissolution* (Princeton, NJ: Princeton University Press, 1997). Wide-ranging analysis of aspects of the 'dissolution' of the GDR.

*[131]   A. J. McAdams, *Germany Divided* (Princeton, NJ: Princeton University Press, 1993). Clear account of German–German relations.

[132]   L. H. McFalls, *Communism's Collapse, Democracy's Demise?* (Basingstoke: Macmillan, 1995).

[133]   P. H. Merkl (ed.), *The Federal Republic of Germany at 45: Union without Unity* (Basingstoke: Macmillan, 1995).

[134]   A. J. Merritt and R. L. Merritt (eds), *Public Opinion in Occupied Germany: The OMGUS Surveys, 1945–49* (Urbana: University of Illinois Press, 1970).

[135]   M. Mertes, S. Müller and H. A. Winkler, *In Search of Germany* (New Brunswick: Transaction Publishers, 1996).

[136]   S. Meuschel, *Legitimation und Parteiherrschaft* (Frankfurt-on-Main: Suhrkamp, 1992).

[137]   Meyer, *Die Machtelite in der Ära Honecker* (Tübingen: A. Francke Verlag, 1991).

[138]   S. Miller and H. Potthoff, *A History of German Social Democracy* (Leamington Spa: Berg, 1986).

[139]   A. Mitter and S. Wolle (eds), *'Ich liebe euch doch alle!' Befehle und Lageberichte des MfS, Jan.–Nov. 1989* (Berlin: BasisDruck, 1990).

[140]   A. Mitter and S. Wolle, *Untergang auf Raten* (Munich: C. Bertelsmann Verlag, 1993). Already a classic text of 'politically engaged' East German historians, presenting a 'decline and fall' thesis of the GDR as already 'on the skids' from 1953 onwards – an interpretation less evident in Wolle's more recent *Die heile Welt der Diktatur: Alltag und Herrschaft in der DDR* (Berlin: Ch. Links, 1998).

[141]   N. Edwina Moreton (ed.), *Germany between East and West* (Cambridge: Cambridge University Press, 1987).

105

*[142]   N. Naimark, *The Russians in Germany* (Cambridge, Mass.: Harvard University Press, 1995). Detailed account of the Soviet occupation of East Germany, based on Soviet as well as German archives, with chapters on topics ranging from rape and robbery, through the kidnapping of German scientists, to the reception of Russian high culture.

[143]   E. Neubert, *Geschichte der Opposition in der DDR, 1949–1989* (Berlin: Ch. Links Verlag, 1997). Encyclopedic compendium from a former East German theologian and sociologist.

[144]   A. J. Nicholls, *Freedom with Responsibility* (Oxford: Oxford University Press, 1995). Detailed account of the origins and early years of the West German 'social market economy'.

*[145]   A. J. Nicholls, *The Bonn Republic: West German Democracy 1945–1990* (London: Longman, 1997). Clear, balanced introduction.

[146]   L. Niethammer, A. von Plato and D. Wierling, *Die volkseigene Erfahrung* (Berlin: Rowohlt, 1991). Intriguing oral history interviews conducted in the GDR in 1987.

[147]   E. Noelle and E. P. Neumann, *Jahrbuch der Öffentlichen Meinung* (Allensbach: Verlag für Demoskopie, series, 1956–). Superb source for number-crunching analyses of West German public opinion over the decades (including united Germany).

[148]   B. Ruhm von Oppen (ed.), *Documents on Germany under Occupation, 1945–55* (London: Oxford University Press, 1955).

*[149]   J. Osmond (ed.), *German Reunification* (Harlow: Longman, 1992).

[150]   Robin Ostow, *Jews in Contemporary East Germany* (London: Macmillan, 1989). Interviews with selected East German Jews whose controlled interviews (under GDR conditions) still reveal much.

[151]   W. Paterson and G. Smith (eds), *The West German Model: Perspectives on a Stable State* (London: Frank Cass, 1981). Typical collection of essays on the whole admiring aspects of West German success story.

[152]   R. Pommerin (ed.), *The American Impact on Postwar Germany* (Providence, RI: Berghahn, 1995).

[153]   N. Pronay and K. Wilson (eds), *The Political Re-education of Germany and her Allies after World War II* (London: Croom Helm, 1985).

*[154]   P. Pulzer, *German Politics 1945–1995* (Oxford: Oxford University Press, 1995). Short, clear introduction for students (cf also [145]).

[155]   J. Roesler, 'The rise and fall of the planned economy in the German Democratic Republic, 1945–89', *German History*, vol. 9 (1991), pp. 46–61.

[156]   M. Roseman, *Recasting the Ruhr, 1945–1958* (Oxford: Berg, 1992).

[157]   M. Roseman (ed.), *Generations in Conflict* (Cambridge: Cambridge University Press, 1995). An original and stimulating collection with some seminal essays throwing light on important but as yet under-researched aspects of German history.

[158]   M. Sabrow and P. T. Walther (eds), *Historische Forschung und Sozialistische Diktatur* (Leipzig: Leipziger Universitätsverlag, 1995).

[159]   G. Schabowski, *Das Politbüro* (Hamburg: Rowohlt, 1990).

[160]   G. Schabowski, *Der Absturz* (Berlin: Rowohlt, 1991). Intriguing views of a seminal insider (he whose failure to glance adequately at a note in a press conference led to the unexpectedly sudden and uncontrolled fall of the Wall . . .).

[161]   A. Schildt and A. Sywottek (eds), *Modernisierung im Wiederaufbau. Die westdeutsche Gesellschaft der 50er Jahre* (Bonn: Dietz, 1993).

[162]   K. Schroeder, *Geschichte und Transformation des SED-Staates* (Berlin: Akademie Verlag, 1994). This and Schroeder's more recent, informative but tendentious *Der SED-Staat 1949–1990* (Munich: Carl Hanser Verlag, 1998) provide key texts illustrating the remarkable West German resurrection of theories of totalitarianism to apply to the GDR.

[163]   C. Schüddekopf (ed.), *'Wir sind das Volk!'* (Hamburg: Rowohlt, 1990).

[164]   E. Schulin (ed.), *Deutsche Geschichtswissenschaft nach dem zweiten Weltkrieg (1945–1965)* (Munich: Oldenbourg, 1989).

[165]   W. Schulze, *Deutsche Geschichtswissenschaft nach 1945* (Munich: Oldenbourg, 1989). This and [164] re-evaluate early postwar West German historiography.

[166]   H. P. Schwarz, *Konrad Adenauer*, 2 vols (Providence, RI: Berghahn, 1995, 1997). English translation of a classic German interpretation of West Germany's immensely important and controversial first chancellor.

*[167] C. C. Schweitzer *et al.* (eds), *Politics and Government in the Federal Republic of Germany: Basic Documents* (Leamington Spa: Berg, 1984). Useful set of original documents in translation.

[168]   Harry Shaffer, *Women in the Two Germanies* (New York: Pergamon 1981).

[169]   E. Owen Smith, *The German Economy* (London: Routledge, 1994).

[170]   G. Smith, *Democracy in Western Germany* (Aldershot: Gower, 3rd edn, 1986).

*[171] G. Smith, W. Paterson and Peter H. Merkl (eds), *Developments in West German Politics* (London: Macmillan, 1989).

*[172] G. Smith, W. Paterson, P. H. Merkl and S. Padgett (eds), *Developments in German Politics* (Basingstoke: Macmillan, 1992).

*[173] G. Smith, W. Paterson, P. H. Merkl and S. Padgett (eds), *Developments in German Politics 2* (Basingstoke: Macmillan, 1996). This and its predecessors ([171] and [172]) contain a

selection of important and informative articles; very useful for teaching.

[174]   F. Spotts, *The Churches and Politics in Germany* (Middletown, Conn.: Wesleyan University Press, 1973).

[175]   D. Staritz, *Geschichte der DDR, 1949–1990* (Frankfurt: Suhrkamp, 1996). Updated version of useful 1985 guide.

[176]   *Statistisches Jahrbuch der DDR* (Berlin: Staatsverlag der DDR, annually).

[177]   R. Steininger, *Deutsche Geschichte 1945–61*, 2 vols (Frankfurt: Fischer, 2nd edn, 1996).

[178]   S. Szabo, *The Diplomacy of German Unification* (New York: St Martin's Press, 1992). Blow by blow chronicle of moves by 'key players'; little analysis of wider conditions of unification.

*[179]   J. K. A. Thomanek and J. Mellis (eds), *Politics, Society and Government in the German Democratic Republic: Basic Documents* (Oxford, New York, Munich: Berg, 1988). Still useful collection of documents in English.

[180]   H. A. Turner, *Germany from Partition to Reunification* (New Haven, CT: Yale University Press, 1992). Updated version of Turner's *Two Germanies*: generally conservative political narrative with primary focus on West German history.

[181]   I. Turner (ed.), *Reconstruction in Postwar Germany* (Oxford: Berg, 1989).

[182]   S. Verba, 'Germany: the remaking of political culture', in L. Pye and S. Verba, *Political Culture and Political Development* (Princeton, NJ: Princeton University Press, 1965).

[183]   I. Wallace (ed.), *East Germany*, World Bibliographical Series vol. 77 (Oxford: Clio Press, 1987).

[184]   I. Wallace (ed.), *The GDR under Honecker, 1971–81* (Dundee: GDR Monitor Special Series, no. 1, 1981).

[185]   I. Wallace (ed.), *The GDR in the 1980s* (Dundee: GDR Monitor Special Series no. 4, 1984).

[186]   G. Wallraff, *Lowest of the Low* (London: Methuen, 1988).

[187]   H. Weber, *Die DDR 1945–1990* (Munich: Oldenbourg, 1993). Updated version of 1986 classic by the senior West German expert on GDR history.

[188]   H. Weber, *DDR: Dokumente, 1945–1985* (Munich: dtv, 1986).

[189]   I. Wilharm, *Deutsche Geschichte 1962–1983*, 2 vols (Frankfurt: Fischer, 1985).

[190]   Wissenschaftliche Rat für soziologische Forschung in der DDR (ed.), *3. Kongress der Marxistisch-Leninistischen Soziologie: Lebensweise und Sozialstruktur* (Berlin: Dietz-Verlag, 1981). Interesting collection of what East German sociologists could publish about their own society.

[191]   *Wörterbuch der Geschichte* (Berlin: Dietz, 1984).

[192]   *Wörterbuch der Marxistisch–Leninistischen Soziologie* (Berlin: Dietz, 1977). This and [191] represent official GDR views on various concepts in history and sociology.

*[193] R. Woods, *Opposition in the GDR under Honecker, 1971–85* (London: Macmillan, 1986). Still a good English-language guide to selected aspects of East German opposition, particularly dissident intelligentsia, although there is a lot more which can now be said (see particularly [143]).

[194] P. Zelikow and C. Rice, *Germany unified and Europe transformed* (Cambridge, Mass: Harvard University Press, 1995).

[195] H. Zwahr, *Ende einer Selbstzerstörung* (Göttingen: Vandenhoeck and Ruprecht, 1993). Account of revolutionary autumn from the perspective of a (nineteenth-century specialist) East German historian in Leipzig as it happened.

Index

113